DIE WEHRMACHT IN KAMPF

VITEBSK

The Fight and Destruction of the Third Panzer Army

OTTO HEIDKÄMPER

Translated by
LINDEN LYONS

CASEMATE

Philadelphia & Oxford

AN AUSA BOOK
Published in the United States of America and Great Britain in 2017 by
CASEMATE PUBLISHERS
1950 Lawrence Road, Havertown, PA 19083, USA
and
The Old Music Hall, 106–108 Cowley Road, Oxford OX4 1JE, UK

Hardback edition: ISBN 978-1-61200-548-5
Digital edition: ISBN 978-1-61200-549-2

Cataloging-in-publication data is available from the Library of Congress and
the British Library.

Printed and bound in the United States of America

For a complete list of Casemate titles, please contact:

CASEMATE PUBLISHERS (US)
Telephone (610) 853-9131
Fax (610) 853-9146
Email: casemate@casematepublishers.com
www.casematepublishers.com

CASEMATE PUBLISHERS (UK)
Telephone (01865) 241249
Email: casemate-uk@casematepublishers.co.uk
www.casematepublishers.co.uk

Contents

Foreword

Our knowledge of the apocalyptic battlefields at the Eastern Front is shaped by a number of battles, for instance Moscow, Stalingrad, and Kursk. But these were like icebergs in the ocean, and a lot of fighting took place 'beneath the surface', at other places and times during the years 1941–45. The fighting in the region of Vitebsk between the summer of 1943 and the final destruction of the German forces in the area during the 1944 Soviet summer offensive *Bagration* – the period covered in this book – is a good example of this. This intriguing book sheds light on the actions in this sector of the front.

This volume has to be seen in the context of its creation. It was first published in German in 1954, at a time when NATO was studying the German conduct of war against the Soviets during the Second World War. The tone of the book is very factual and can appear cold; it is clearly that of a general staff officer who is interested in the planning and conduct of operations, and the operational results of tactical actions, but who has less interest in the human dimension and the human suffering. While this is true for the account of the German side, it is even more so for the Soviets. For instance, the author comments on the threat that the Partisans (or 'Bandits', as he refers to them, in line with German terminology of the Second World War) posed to the Germans. What Otto Heidkämper fails to address is the question as to why there was a growing Partisan threat in the German hinterland, which was largely a consequence of the brutal German occupation. One reason for this failure might be the fact that Heidkämper was a member of the 'new breed' of officers who were closely associated with the Nazi system and its ideology. Heidkämper, who ended the Second World War as Lieutenant-General and was awarded the Knight's Cross on 8 February 1943, has been called by a German historian the 'embodiment of the warrior of the new *Weltanschauung*'.[1]

Despite this, the book adopts a theme that was typical for German (ex-)military writers of the 1950s and early 1960s: German operational excellence and unrivalled military expertise were undermined by Hitler's interference in operational matters. Heidkämper expresses this view very strongly. There was more than a kernel of truth in this assessment, but it can also be argued the generals followed Hitler's orders for too long, often against their better military judgement. This is also a theme that appears throughout the book, though probably unintentionally on the part of the author.

When Heidkämper wrote his book in the 1950s, he did not have the wealth of sources available that historians now have access to. As a consequence, some of his points might not stand up to academic scrutiny. Bearing this in mind, *Vitebsk* offers a fascinating insight into the fighting at this forgotten part of the Eastern Front, through the lens of one of the main actors on the German side. This alone makes this a worthy addition to the plethora of publications on the Second World War.

Dr. Matthias Strohn, M.St., FRHistS
Visiting Fellow, Centre for Historical Analysis and
Conflict Research
Senior Lecturer, Royal Military Academy Sandhurst
Senior Research Fellow, Buckingham University

---

[1]Christian Hartmann, *Wehrmacht im Ostkrieg. Front und militärisches Hinterland 1941/42*, Munich 2010, p. 9.

Maps

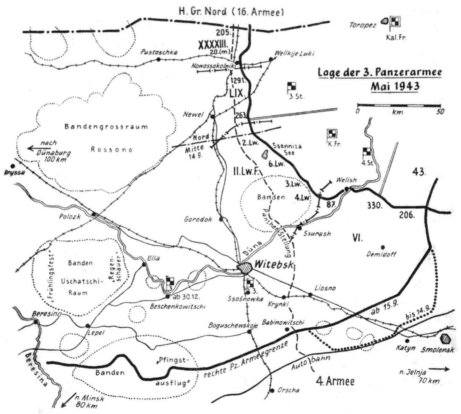

Map 1: Situation of the Third Panzer Army (May 1943)

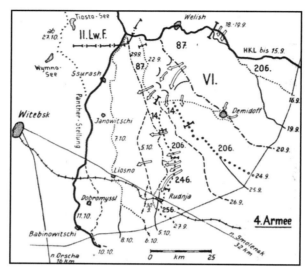

Map 2: Retreat of the VI Corps (16 September–11 October 1943)

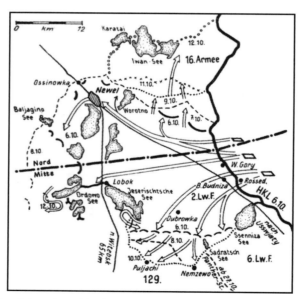

Map 3: Soviet breakthrough at Nevel on 6 October 1943. Development of the situation until 12 October 1943

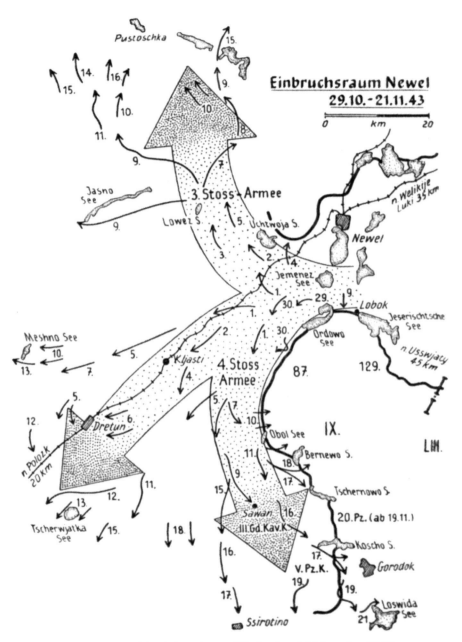

Map 4: Nevel breakthrough area (29 October–21 November 1943)

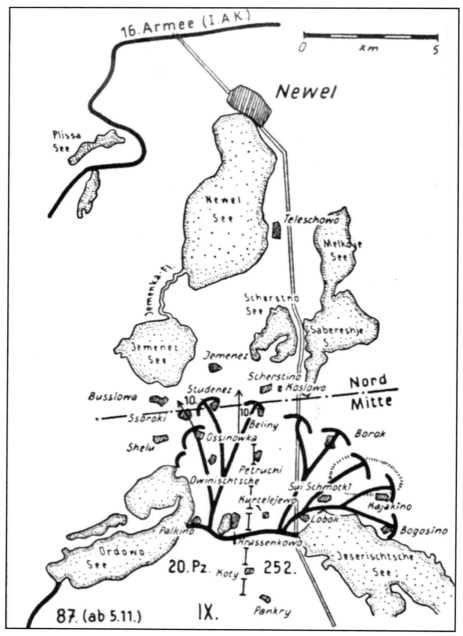

Map 5: Attack from the Lobok sector. Final attempt to close the fatal gap between Army Groups Centre and North (8 November 1943)

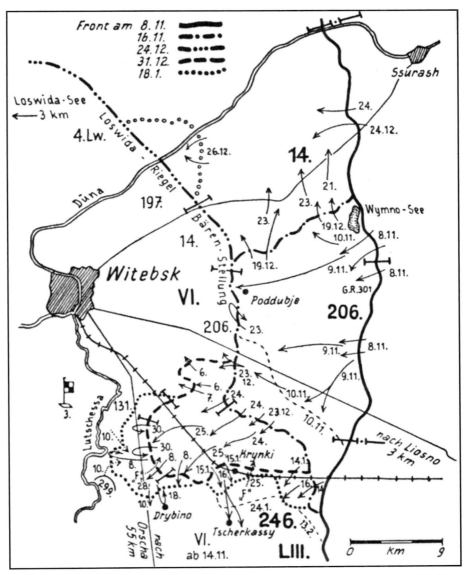

Map 6: Combat east and southeast of Vitebsk (8 November 1943–18 January 1944)

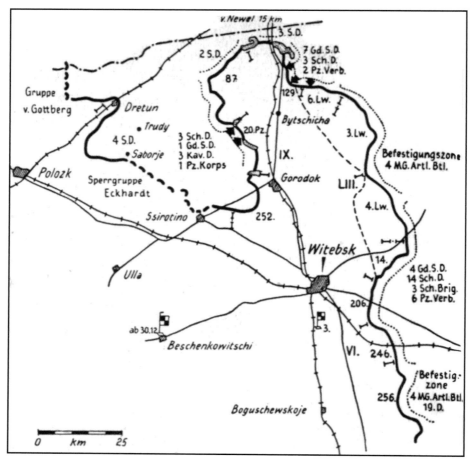

Map 7: Situation of the Third Panzer Army at the beginning of the first winter defensive battle around Vitebsk (13 December 1943)

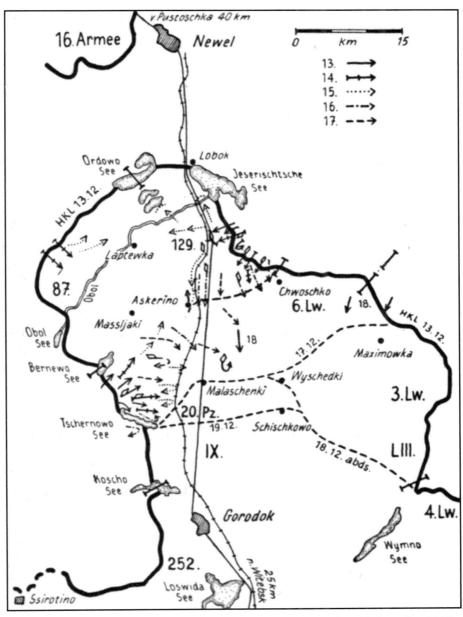

Map 8: Combat on the northern wing of the Third Panzer Army (13–18 December 1943)

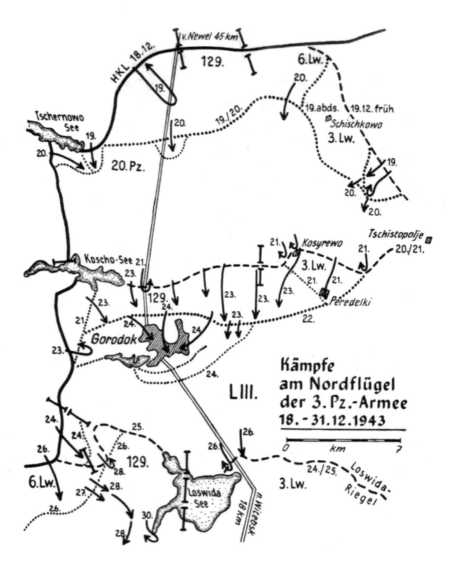

Map 9: Combat on the northern wing of the Third Panzer Army (18–31 December 1943)

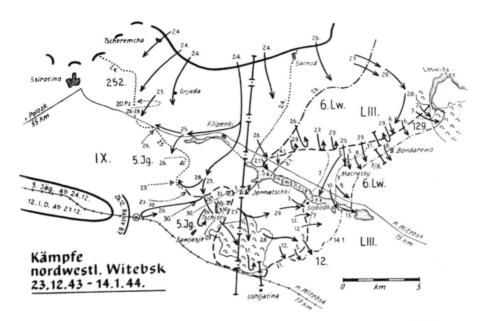

Map 10: Combat northwest of Vitebsk (23 December 1943–14 January 1944)

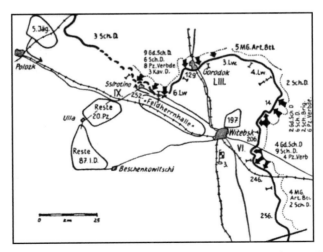

Map 11: Situation of the Third Panzer Army (24 December 1943)

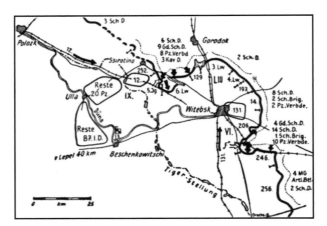

Map 12: Situation of the Third Panzer Army (31 December 1943)

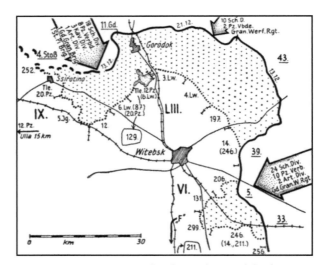

Map 13: Situation on 18 January 1944, after the conclusion of the first winter defensive battle around Vitebsk. Soviet territorial gains in the vicinity of Vitebsk since 13 December 1943

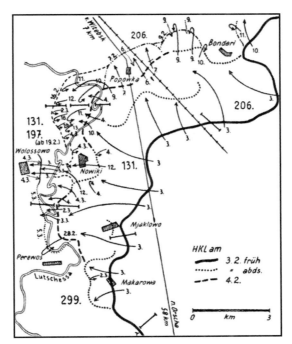

Map 14: Combat deep into the breakthrough area southeast of Vitebsk (3–16 February 1944 and 28 February–5 March 1944)

Map 15: Combat northwest of Vitebsk (3–16 February 1944)

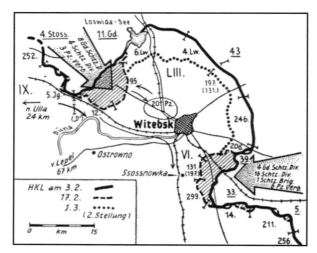

Map 16: *Situation on 17 February 1944, after the conclusion of the second winter defensive battle around Vitebsk. Soviet territorial gains (3–17 February 1944)*

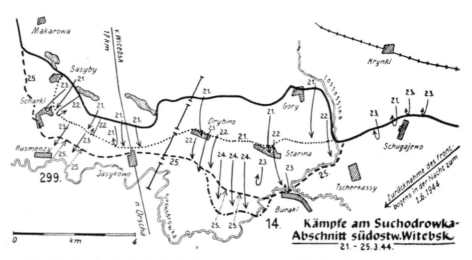

Map 17: *Combat in the Sukhodrovka sector, southeast of Vitebsk (21–25 March 1944)*

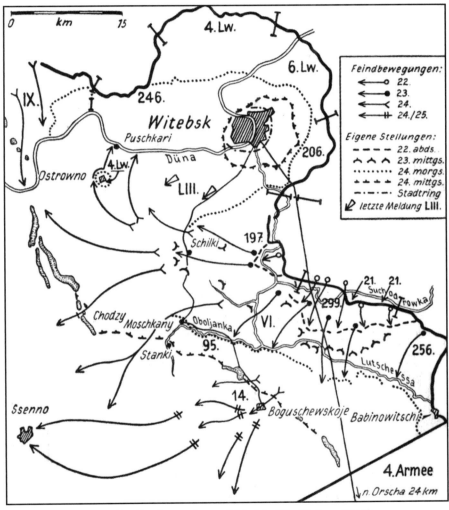

Map 18: Combat southeast of Vitebsk (21–25 June 1944)

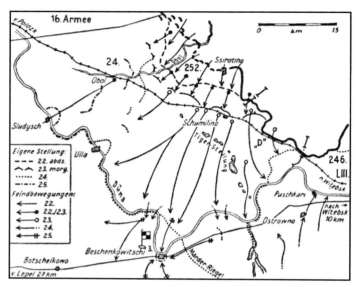

Map 19: Combat northwest of Vitebsk (22–25 June 1944)

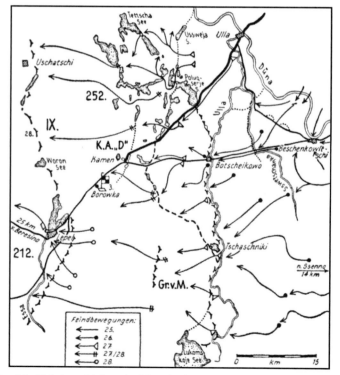

Map 20: Fighting withdrawal of the Third Panzer Army (24–28 June 1944)

Place names:

German	English usage
Babinowitschi	Babinovichi
Baljagino-See	Lake Balyagino
die Beresina	Berezina River (tributary of the Dnieper)
Beresino	Berezino
Bernewo-See	Lake Bernovo
Beschenkowitschi	Beshenkovichi
Boguschewskoje	Bogushevsk
Bol. Budniza	Bolshaya Budnitsa
Bol. Rubiny	Bolshaya Rubiny
Bondarewo	Bondarevo
Borowka	Borovka
Botscheikowo	Bocheikovo
Busslowa	Buslova
Bytschicha	Bychykha
Chodzy	Khodtsy
Chwoschko	Khvoshko
Demidow	Demidov
Dobromyssl	Dobromysli
Drybino	Dribino
Dryssa	Drissa
Dubrowka	Dubrovka
die Düna	Western Dvina River
Gorbatschi	Gorbachi
Grjada	Gryada
Hannover	Hanover
Isjum	Izium
Iwan-See	Lake Ivan
Janowitschi	Yanovichi
Jasno-See	Lake Yazno
Jasykowo	Yazykovo
Jelnja	Yelnya
Jemenez	Emenets
Jemenez-See	Lake Emenets

Jemenka-Fluß	Yemenka River
Jermatschki	Yermachki
Jeserischtsche-See	Lake Ezerishche
Karatai-See	Lake Karatay
Kljasti	Klyastitsy
Koscho-See	Lake Kosho
Kosyrewo	Kozyrevo
Krassenkowo	Kosenkovo
Kurtelejewo	Kurteleyevo
Kusmenzy	Kusmentsy
Laptewka	Laptevka
Liosno	Liozno
Loswida-See	Lake Losvida
Lowez-See	Lake Lovets
Lukomskoje-See	Lake Lukomlskoye
die Lutschessa	Luchesa River
Makarowa	Makarova
Malaschenki	Malashenki
Massljaki	Maslyaki
Maximowka	Maksimovka
Melkoje-See	Lake Melkoye
Mjaklowo	Myaklovo
Moschkany	Moshkany
Nemzewo	Nemtsevo
Newel	Nevel
Newel-See	Lake Nevel
Nowiki	Noviki
Nowossokolniki	Novosokolniki
die Oboljanka	Obolyanka River
Ordowo-See	Lake Ordovo
Orechi-See	Lake Orekhi
Orscha	Orsha
Ossinowka	Osinovka
Ostrowno	Ostrovno
Owinischtsche	Ovinishche

Perewos	Peravoz
Poddubje	Poddubye
Poluoserje-See	Lake Polozerye
Polozk	Polotsk
Popowka	Popovka
Puljachi	Pulyakhi
Puschkari	Pushkari
Pustoschka	Pustoshka
Rossedenje	Rossedenye
Rudnja	Rudnya
Sabereshje-See	Lake Zaverezhye
Sachod	Zakhody
Sadratsch-See	Lake Sadrach
Saronowskoje-See	Lake Zaronovskoye
Sawan	Zavan
Sawjasje	Zavyazye
Scharki	Sharki
Scherstno-See	Lake Cherstno
Schilki	Shilki
Schischkovo	Shishkovo
Schugajewo	Shugayevo
Schumilino	Shumilino
Ssenniza-See	Lake Sennitsa
Ssenno	Senno
Ssirotino	Sirotino
Ssludysch	Sludysh
Ssosnowka	Sosnovka
Ssurash	Surazh
Staroje Sselo	Staroye Syalo
Stepankowa	Stepankova
Studenez	Studenets
die Suchodrowka	Sukhodrovka River
Sui Schmotki	Zui Shmotki
die Swetschanka	Svechanka River
Teleschowo	Teleshovo

Tettscha-See	Lake Tetcha
Toropez	Toropets
Tschaschniki	Chashniki
Tscheremcha	Cheremkha
Tscherkassy	Cherkassy
Tschernowo-See	Lake Chernovo
Tscherwjatka-See	Lake Chervyatka
Tschisti	Chystsi
Tschistopolje	Chistopolye
Uchtwoja-See	Lake Usvoya
Ulla	Ula
Uschatschi	Ushatshi
Uschatschi-Raum	Ushatshi (bandit) territory
Ushljatina	Uzhlyatsina
Ussweja-See	Lake Usveya
Usswjaty	Usvyaty
Welikije Luki	Velikiye Luki
Welish	Velizh
Witebsk	Vitebsk
Woltschij Gory	Volchi Gory
Wolossowo	Volosovo
Woron-See	Lake Voron
Worotno-See	Lake Vorotno
Wymno-See	Lake Vymno
Wyschedki	Vyshedki

In memory of the soldiers of the Third Panzer Army who fell at Vitebsk.

O.H.

CHAPTER I

The combat situation of the Third Panzer Army in the summer of 1943

In early May 1943, a Fieseler Storch brought me from Smolensk to the headquarters of the Third Panzer Army in Sosnovka, 10 kilometres south of Vitebsk. On the way, we circled a few times around Katyn. The Polish officers murdered there by the Soviets had been discovered a few days previously in the presence of an international commission. There was young birch forest all around. Lying around the edges of several pits were probably 200 to 300 disinterred bodies.

After another 20 minutes, we flew over the rubble and ruins of the city where in little more than one year the fate of the Third Panzer Army would be decided: Vitebsk. Previously inhabited by 170,000 people, the regional capital of White Ruthenia had been set ablaze by Young Communists immediately before its capture by German troops in the summer of 1941. Only a few church steeples remained standing amidst what was otherwise devastated land.

I reported to Colonel-General Georg-Hans Reinhardt in the afternoon. He had commanded the Third Panzer Army for over one-and-a-half years, and I was to be his new chief of staff.

Employed on the left wing of Army Group Centre, the Third Panzer Army stood along a curved, northeastward-facing frontline of more than 250 kilometres. The right wing of the panzer army adjoined the Fourth Army northeast of Demidov, whilst the left wing adjoined the Sixteenth Army (under Army Group North) northwest of Velikiye Luki.

The length of this front was exactly the same as the distance between Berlin and Hanover.

For the defence of this sector of the front, the following units were subordinated to the Third Panzer Army: the VI Corps with three divisions, the II Luftwaffe Field Corps with four Luftwaffe field divisions, the LIX Corps with two divisions, and the XLIII Corps with two divisions. In panzer army reserve was the 83rd Infantry Division, and in army group reserve in the area of the panzer army was the 8th Panzer Division. In May, both divisions were engaged in local anti-partisan operations northeast of Vitebsk, although in July the latter would be withdrawn; the former would be committed in the vicinity of the XLIII Corps following the withdrawal of the 20th Motorised Infantry Division. During this time, the Third Panzer Army had provisions for 292,000 men.

After a fierce struggle during the winter, the fighting on the front had gradually, over a period of approximately two months, frozen into static warfare. Partisans were our main concern at this time – the entire rear area of the panzer army was infested with them. Due to their merciless brutality, we saw them not as regular troops but as bandits. They wreaked havoc right up to the front, and not a day passed without fatalities caused by bandit raids, mines, or shootings from behind. The threat posed by large bandit territories in the rear area of the panzer army meant that just one supply route from the west via Polotsk was available, and it could only be used by day, and under escort. The shortage of personnel in the panzer army prevented the possibility of sweeping operations against bandits; smaller operations brought only local and temporary relief. We were particularly worried about how to deal with them in the event of a resurgence of large-scale fighting on the frontline.

In the following months, combat activity remained relatively quiet in comparison to other sectors of the front. Nevertheless, daily raids and patrol operations consumed so many forces that the high command of the Third Panzer Army repeatedly reported its concerns to Army Group Centre. During the course of 17 raids and 1324 patrol operations carried out in June, our troops ensured that we remained constantly informed about the enemy.

Heavy losses were inflicted upon us by two major enemy operations, one in late May and early June at Velizh (in the area of the VI Corps) and the other in late June and early July to the northeast of Nevel (in the sector of the LIX Corps). The enemy, as expected, was becoming active again on both sides of Vitebsk.

In a meeting with the commander of Army Group Centre, Field-Marshal Günther von Kluge, in Smolensk on 17 June, Reinhardt pointed out that the rapid deterioration of our combat strength would weaken our ability to resist a Soviet attack. The most likely location for such as attack was the westward-protruding salient covered by the Third Panzer Army. Of course, while the immediate objective would be Vitebsk, with its road and railway junction, the long-term objectives were Dünaburg and Riga. 'We'll help you if that turns out to be the case', said Kluge, who, it should be noted, did not actually believe that the panzer army was in peril. Reinhardt then brought up the inadequate training of the four Luftwaffe field divisions, which were receiving no replacements whatsoever and thus becoming weaker every day. 'I cannot help', replied Kluge. 'At the moment, anything that's not absolutely essential for us is urgently needed for the creation of a European reserve. *Citadel* is now approved, and from tomorrow it must be able to be unleashed at any time within the next eight days.[1] We must be clear that this will be *the* battle of the year. Otherwise, we're agreed that it would be ideal if the Russian were to reveal his own intentions by making the first move.'

Afterwards, the disjointed frontline leadership on the boundary with Army Group North in Novosokolniki came up. The high command of the panzer army had already reported on this in writing: we wanted to withdraw our left wing to the northwest of Novosokolniki, where we would command high ground. Unfortunately, Army Group North rejected this proposal on the grounds that it would have an adverse effect upon their right wing. Weeks of debate followed, which eventually led to a disastrous shift of the line of demarcation between the two army groups.

---

[1] 'Citadel' was the code name for the great pincer attack against the Kursk salient by Army Group South from the vicinity of Belgorod and by the Ninth Army (Army Group Centre) from the Orel salient.

On 14 September, the High Command of the Army (OKH) ordered that the new line would extend from east to west about 12 kilometres to the south of Nevel. This situation would later be rectified.

At the conclusion of the above-mentioned meeting, Reinhardt once more emphasised the probability of a major winter offensive by the Soviets against the Third Panzer Army. It was here that the front stretched furthest to the west, enabling an attack in the direction of Dünaburg. Kluge agreed, but argued that the Russians would be weakened after being defeated in *Citadel*. 'Moreover,' he continued, 'though we may be facing certain difficulties, the Russians are too, and to a much greater extent. We're constantly receiving news about their transportation difficulties, their serious shortage of personnel, and their extraordinary lack of rations for the Russian population.'

Citadel commenced on 5 July. After some initial success, the attack lost momentum. The Soviets launched a counteroffensive on 11 July against the Orel salient (the area of the Second Panzer Army) from the east and from the north. *Citadel* finally came to a standstill on 13 July, and by 16 July the terrain that we had gained had to be relinquished. On 23 July, the entire Eastern Front was ablaze and on the verge of collapsing due to strong Soviet attacks on the Kuban and Mius Rivers, as well as near the cities of Izium, Orel, and Leningrad.

Memorandum on the conduct of a winter defensive battle in the sector of the Third Panzer Army

At first, the Third Panzer Army remained unaffected by the major battles that had arisen everywhere. However, the concern about what would come induced the high command of the panzer army to present to Army Group Centre on 7 August a 'Memorandum on the conduct of a winter defensive battle in the sector of the Third Panzer Army'. We strongly expressed the view that, once the present fighting had drawn to a close, a major Soviet operation in the general direction of Dünaburg was to be expected. The base of this operation was likely to be sought on the left flank of the Third Panzer Army and on the right flank of Army Group North. The operational goal of isolating Army Group North with an advance on Riga would be easiest to achieve from this base, as it was here that the front stretched furthest west. In combination with such an operation, the Russians would undoubtedly want to neutralise the supply to the left wing of Army Group Centre. They would attempt to do this by rapidly taking Vitebsk, with its road and railway junction, or by piercing the right wing of the panzer army in the direction of the Vitebsk–Smolensk and Orsha–Smolensk railway lines. We presumed that the focal point of the Soviet operation would lie between Novosokolniki and Lake Sennitsa (30 kilometres to the southeast of Nevel). From here, the enemy would quickly come into possession of Nevel, of the local road junction, and of the railway lines leading into the city from the north and northeast.

Even if it should transpire that the enemy would become incapable of advancing on Dünaburg, it was our view that he would still attack with limited objectives. The occupation of Vitebsk and Nevel alone would have impacted decisively upon the supply to the Third Panzer Army. In any case, we believed that the panzer army would have to be prepared for a great defensive battle.

In this memorandum, one division per 15-kilometre defensive front was regarded as acceptable. However, our forces were currently spread too thinly in the main defensive area. Each division, low in combat strength, held an approximately 25-kilometre front. For several divisions, there was only one man for every 50 to 80 metres of front trench. Reserves were lacking completely.

Finally, the headquarters of the panzer army requested five additional infantry divisions, an extra panzer or panzer-grenadier division, reinforced artillery, antitank weapons, pioneers, and construction forces.

This memorandum was significant and is described here in detail, as it forewarned what was to become the reality in the course of the next eleven months: the penetration of Nevel, the winter defensive battles around Vitebsk, and the Soviet offensive in the direction of Dünaburg that strangulated Army Group North.

Impending battle (Map 1)

Meanwhile, the situation in the large Orel salient had developed so unfavourably that its evacuation by 18 August was ordered. The rest of

Army Group Centre became embroiled in the heavy defensive fighting brought about by this withdrawal.

It continued to be comparatively quiet on the front of the Third Panzer Army, although raids by both sides did increase in strength and frequency, leading to days of heavy, costly battles. The rear area of the panzer army was by no means calm. Night-time flights of up to 100 enemy aircraft steadily supplied the large bandit territory of Rossono, demonstrating the close association of the Red Army with the bandits. Within four days, 3,229 railway lines in the rear area were blown up by bandits. It was with increasing urgency that we reported by telegraph, by telephone, and in person the danger confronting the panzer army.

In principle, the army group agreed with our memorandum. But instead of being supplied with new forces, we were required to hand over, one after the other, the LIX Corps, the 330th and 291st Infantry Divisions, some battalions, and army artillery.

The monthly situation reports by our divisions to the army group had once again made quite clear the defencelessness of the Third Panzer Army given its present composition and shortage of manpower. Field-Marshal von Kluge wrote to the OKH about this: 'The morale of the troops is affected by heavy losses and by the noticeable superiority of the enemy in materiel and personnel. Listlessness is becoming more frequent, but there is no sign of disobedience. The spirit and attitude of the Russian troops have been unmistakeably lifted by their successes during the summer.'

The daily reports we received showed that the southern and central sectors of the Eastern Front were in turmoil and that everything was in a state of flux. For weeks, the enemy advanced despite the tremendous effort of the German soldier. Every day, we became more anxious about what might happen. The large gaps in the front somehow had to be closed so as to prevent its collapse.

East of Smolensk, the Soviets reached Yelnya by 30 August, prompting a serious crisis arose that was likely to have a detrimental effect on the Third Panzer Army. It now became apparent that, since 5 July, the Soviets had constantly been able to replenish their units. On our side, the same soldiers were still fighting. Their ranks were thinning alarmingly.

They had given their all, but many could no longer do so. To make matters worse, there was always the distressing news of the bombing of the Fatherland.

During this time, it was clear that a major Soviet offensive would occur in the near future. The enemy conducted local attacks against the VI Corps (under General of Infantry Hans Jordan) on the right wing of the panzer army and against the II Luftwaffe Field Corps (under General of Air Troops Alfred Schlemm) to the east of Nevel. Furthermore, the bandits in the hinterland were amply supplied by air. The development of the situation for our southern neighbour, the Fourth Army, made it increasingly likely that the withdrawal of the right wing of the panzer army would have to be carried out earlier than intended. Despite this, the panzer army would still be compelled to relinquish control of some of its forces. Ration strength on 6 September was enough for 230,000 men, yet our combat strength had decreased even further as a result of the complete absence of replacements for our losses.

The Soviets were in a strong position and often triumphant. We were uncertain as to the continuing reliability of the so-called Eastern Troops, 20,000 of whom were in the panzer army alone![2] The number of deserters amongst them was growing, and the Russian population was also becoming uneasy due to the ever-approaching front. They were indifferent – even defiant – in response to our arrangements.

The construction of the Panther Line (Map 1)

At the end of August, the army group ordered an investigation by the high command of the Third Panzer Army into the establishment of a new defensive line that would roughly extend from Babinovichi, to the northeast of Surazh, to the east of Nevel, and then further to the north. This 'Panther Line' was to be constructed as quickly as possible so that it would, by 1 November, be capable of withstanding concentrated Soviet attacks. The right wing of the panzer army would need to be able to

---

[2]Translator's note: The Eastern Troops consisted of Russian conscripts and volunteers in the German military.

retreat to this line should the situation of the rest of the army group necessitate it. To this end, on 2 September we ordered as a matter of urgency the commencement of construction in those regions where the enemy would focus his attention: Vitebsk, Nevel, and on either side of the railway leading westwards from Novosokolniki. We particularly placed emphasis on the building of antitank obstacles east of Nevel. Construction would at first be carried out by elements of the Todt Organisation.[3]

The relocation of the left boundary of the army group (Map 1)

In concern over what was to come, on 14 September the OKH ordered that the boundary between Army Groups Centre and North be relocated to an east–west line approximately 12 kilometres to the south of Nevel. This meant that the Third Panzer Army had to give up its command of the XLIII Corps (with the 263rd, 83rd, and 205th Infantry Divisions). In a telephone conversation with Kluge on the evening of 13 September, Reinhardt had already advised against the new demarcation on the grounds that it would divide German leadership in the anticipated battle zone. Our thoughts on the shift of the boundary were also submitted in writing to the army group on the same evening. Nonetheless, the OKH order for the transfer of the XLIII Corps was issued the following afternoon. We had repeatedly stressed the disadvantages of having an army group boundary running through the middle of what we foresaw as a major wintertime battle area (south of Nevel, to north of Novosokolniki), and we did so one last time at a conference with the army group on 13 September. All in vain! To our horror, the OKH decided against us. All our warnings had been ignored. The II Luftwaffe Field Corps was now on the boundary of the army group. This corps was well-equipped but green, with only a handful of trained leaders in the weak 2nd Luftwaffe Field Division. There would soon be dire consequences!

---

[3]Translator's note: The Todt Organisation was responsible for many, predominantly military, engineering projects in Nazi Germany and occupied Europe.

Enemy forces on the front of the Third Panzer Army (Map 1)

But, at that moment, we were more concerned about the withdrawal on the right wing of the panzer army, which had been made necessary by the development of the situation to our south.

Before turning our attention to this matter, it is best to become acquainted with the organisation, strength, and condition of those forces of the Red Army that stood on the opposite side of the front of the Third Panzer Army.

We faced the Kalinin Front, the headquarters of which lay in Toropets. It comprised the 3rd Shock Army, with its left wing on the heights of Nevel; the 4th Shock Army, with its left wing approximately 18 kilometres east of Velizh; and the 43rd Army, of which only parts stood opposite the right wing of the VI Corps. In mid-September, the 3rd Shock Army had at its disposal two rifle and two guards rifle divisions, two rifle brigades, and two separate machine-gun battalions; the 4th Shock Army had five rifle divisions, a rifle brigade, and a machine-gun artillery brigade; the 43rd Army had two or three rifle divisions opposing the VI Corps. We did not regard these forces to be particularly combat effective, because they lacked replacements for their considerable losses during the positional warfare of the summer. Even so, the many hostile raids and local attacks over the summer, involving vast expenditure of ammunition, convinced us that the enemy, whilst concealing his true intentions, sought to gain points of reference for his planned major offensive.

CHAPTER 2

The retreat on the right wing of the Third Panzer Army

On 16 September, in order to maintain contact with the retreating Fourth Army, the extreme right wing of the VI Corps also withdrew. Any withdrawal under enemy pressure is one of the most difficult of military operations, requiring meticulous preparation and demanding thereafter the utmost effort from soldiers and commanders. Yet the difficulties arising from the withdrawal of the right wing of the panzer army were bound to increase dramatically in the near future. It had to be carried out approximately 14 days earlier than scheduled, so that our forces could avoid being overrun by the enemy. While the right wing retreated up to 22 kilometres in a single night, it was rapidly approaching a point where it would have to stand firm.

On the night of 15/16 September, about 27 kilometres of the old front on the right wing of the VI Corps was abandoned in a 12-kilometre withdrawal. Three weeks of the toughest defensive combat had commenced, demanding from our troops far more than could ordinarily be expected. The Soviets were in immediate pursuit, attempting with assaults of regimental strength to disrupt the orderliness of our withdrawal and to prevent any retreat elsewhere.

Velizh, which for months had been fiercely fought over between friend and foe, was given up on 20 September. Demidov was relinquished on 22 September. In the forests to the south of these towns, both sides suffered heavy losses. On this day, the retreating divisions (the

206th and 87th Infantry Divisions) faced the powerful enemy offensive along a roughly 90-kilometre front. The first relief troops of the 14th Infantry Division, which was subordinate to the panzer army, arrived in the area of the VI Corps. The division was inserted between the 206th and 87th Infantry Divisions on the following day.

By 15 September, five to six Soviet rifle divisions, one rifle brigade, and one machine-gun artillery brigade had been detected before the two divisions of the VI Corps. By 22 September, these enemy forces had increased to seven rifle divisions, two rifle brigades, a mechanised brigade, an antitank brigade, and a tank regiment. The VI Corps had received no reinforcements or replacements up to this time. By 25 September, the enemy had been further reinforced not only by parts of the 39th Soviet Army, but also by those parts of the 43rd Soviet Army that had previously been fighting the Fourth Army. He then concentrated his forces to the east of Surazh, to the east of Yanovichi, and on both sides of the Vitebsk–Smolensk road. His objective was undoubtedly to exploit the temporary weakness brought about by our retreat, so that he could break through our lines and advance on Vitebsk. Our retreat continually compelled him to redeploy his troops, though his pursuit was surprisingly quick. He rapidly prepared and launched his attacks, frequently penetrating our lines in heavy fighting. This contributed to the series of crises we encountered.

Some degree of relief was provided by the aforementioned arrival of the 14th Infantry Division on 23 September, and by that of the 256th and 246th Infantry Divisions on 27 September. The latter two had come from the Fourth Army and were used to reinforce a large sector of the VI Corps.

On 28 and 29 September, the enemy concentrated his heavy attacks on Rudnya, and on the area to its north. He threw many tanks against us in a number of violent battles, but the 256th Infantry Division, supported by the air force, managed to prevent an enemy breakthrough on the Vitebsk–Smolensk road. The troops in the field had by now been fighting non-stop for 14 days and nights, and still the retreating VI Corps (now with five divisions) succeeded in keeping the enemy at bay. The corps continued to do so for the next few days, even though the enemy had, by 4 October, been increased in strength to eleven rifle divisions, three guards rifle divisions, three rifle brigades, two mechanised brigades, one antitank brigade, and one panzer regiment. On 2 October, the 14th Infantry Division became involved in tough close fighting. On 4 and 5 October, the enemy achieved a deep penetration at Rudnya, and we expected that he would push onwards from here towards Liozno. This push started immediately on 6 October. Meanwhile, a situation developed 75 kilometres north of Vitebsk, whose consequences at that moment could not quite be foreseen, but which, as we had long feared, would have a devastating impact upon the upcoming period of battle.

CHAPTER 3

The Soviet penetration at Nevel

A Soviet offensive was just around the corner. From 30 September, we had spotted enemy movements before the left wing of the panzer army and on the boundary with Army Group North (i.e. with the Sixteenth Army). He had been conducting more patrols and raids, and had been reinforcing his fighter and anti-aircraft defences since 4 October. Finally, he had transferred a subdivision of the staff from the Kalinin Front to an area 70 kilometres east-southeast of Nevel. With German aerial reconnaissance obstructed by the weather conditions, the enemy had successfully concealed the form and strength of his assembled troops.

Supported by heavy artillery, rocket batteries, and ground-attack aircraft, the enemy launched a major offensive early on 6 October, with a wide front extending on either side of the vulnerable army group boundary. He struck the inexperienced and only moderately trained 2nd Luftwaffe Field Division and the southern wing of the Sixteenth Army. We stood firm against the first wave of the attack in the sector between Rossedenye and Volchi Gory, but then strong enemy forces, supported by armour and numerous ground-attack aircraft, penetrated the front and advanced to the highway stretching northwest and southeast of Bolshaya Budnitsa. Enemy troops also broke through the front to the north of the army group boundary, whereupon some of them turned southwards to threaten the deep flank of the 2nd Luftwaffe Field Division. In this way, the interdiction front being set up in Bolshaya Budnitsa was lost.

Everything now took place at an alarming rate. Having carried out the breakthrough, the Soviets immediately advanced with three assault groups, each of approximately brigade-level strength, further westwards and southwestwards: the first via Dubrovka to the southern side of Lake Ezerishche, the second in the direction of Lobok, and the third along the Usvyaty–Nevel highway towards Nevel. The combat troops panicked in some places. The enemy advanced more than 20 kilometres non-stop and encountered only the completely surprised elements of our supply services. By the evening, a gap greater than 18 kilometres in width had opened up between the two army groups. A weak defensive line was being established from the southern tip of Lake Sennitsa extending through the southern tip of Lake Ezerishche, to Lake Ordovo, Lake Balyagino, Osinovka, and to the northern edge of Lake Vorotno, and to its east. The advancing Soviet forces now comprised seven rifle divisions, one rifle brigade, and three tank brigades, and it became ominously apparent that they would soon make contact with the Rossono bandits (approximately 10,000 men). We would then be powerless to stop this combined force from pressing on towards Polotsk.

In view of the difficult withdrawal of the right wing of the panzer army, where fierce fighting had continued to take place on this day, we had few forces available that could assist in the vicinity of Nevel. Parts of the 129th Infantry Division already in the area of the panzer army, as well as some artillery, assault guns, and anti-aircraft units, were all that could be sent overnight to the threatened northern wing. These forces were by no means sufficient to close the gap, especially because the 2nd Luftwaffe Field Division had been completely crushed and was without combat value.

At first, there was alarm at the loss of Nevel in Hitler's headquarters. Nonetheless, in the following days we gained the impression that the very clear danger to the army group boundary was not being taken seriously enough by the highest command. Reich Marshal Hermann Göring was the first to intervene personally, and promised rapid assistance to his II Luftwaffe Field Corps. All 500 machines of the Sixth Air Fleet were committed to the breakthrough sector, while two heavy anti-aircraft artillery battalions would join the ground combat units.

This enabled the corps to build a protective front with hastily gathered forces on 7 October, and to use it to halt the renewed enemy advance.

Over the next few days (until 12 October), the Soviets tried to expand their point of penetration to the south and north by reinforcing their current forces with two more rifle divisions. In particular, they sought to push southwards towards Gorodok and Vitebsk. In concert with Soviet forces marching from the east on Vitebsk, their aim was to cause the collapse of the left wing of the Third Panzer Army and to thereby create a sufficiently broad base (Nevel–Vitebsk) for the planned thrust through the Rossono bandit territory into the Baltic region. The thrusts to the south by the 4th Shock Army and to the north by the 3rd Shock Army were brought to a standstill. We had fought hard and had inflicted heavy casualties on the enemy. The Third Panzer Army now held a line running from Lake Sennitsa through Nemtsevo, Pulyakhi, Lake Ezerishche, to the area between Lobok and Lake Ordovo. Meanwhile, by 12 October, the Sixteenth Army had managed to block the enemy along a line starting four kilometres northwest of Nevel, extending to Lake Karatay and Lake Ivan, and then from there further northeastwards. Surprisingly, the Soviets did not proceed to pierce the weak German defensive line to the west, even though they could have attempted to do so with strong forces in order to reach bandit territory. We assumed that the reason for this was that they intended to expand their point of penetration further to the south and north until a decisive blow could be dealt well into the rear of the panzer army. In fact, in the battles of the following year it turned out that the Soviets would pursue a different objective with regard to the bandits. As soon as the German front had been driven back, the bandits had been ordered further westwards. They would create renewed unrest behind our lines, threatening our supply and combat troops.

Futile attempts to deal with the breakthrough at Nevel (Map 3)

The situation as it had developed in the vicinity of Nevel urgently needed to be resolved before the Soviets could make further gains. We were under the impression that even the enemy had been surprised by his rapid penetration of the front on 6 October, whereby he took Nevel by noon, and that he lacked sufficient forces to exploit this success for a real breakthrough in depth. All the more urgent at this stage were our own countermeasures for retaking at least Nevel and the Nevel–Vitebsk road and thus re-establishing secure contact with the Sixteenth Army. Colonel-General Reinhardt had already spoken with Colonel-General Kurt Zeitzler, the chief of the general staff of the army, about this on 9 October. On the next day, the situation had calmed a little. The IX Corps, the 20th Panzer Division, and a Tiger battalion were put under the command of the panzer army. Reinhardt thereupon requested from Field-Marshal von Kluge that he be given the task of striking against the Nevel breakthrough area in conjunction with elements of the Sixteenth Army. Kluge did not approve this, as he believed the Sixteenth Army to be unfavourably placed.

Enemy reinforcements arrived in the breakthrough area in the next few days. Because of this, Reinhardt repeated his request when he met with Kluge on 13 October at the command post of the IX Corps (commanded by General of the Infantry Erich-Heinrich Clößner and, as of the previous day, responsible for all of the forces deployed on the northern front of the panzer army). Again, Kluge hesitated. He was in doubt as to whether he could spare the 20th Panzer Division for an attack.

On the following day, we learnt that Reinhardt's request had again been rejected. Reinhardt, who visited our combat troops from day to day, from dawn to dusk, both on the northern front and east of Vitebsk, spoke at length with Kluge one evening over the telephone in yet another attempt to gain his permission for an attack by the panzer army. He repeatedly pointed out that any postponement of the attack against the enemy, who was continually being reinforced, would diminish the prospects of success. He added that the situation certainly could not be allowed to stay the way it was in view of the approaching period of mud, and then winter. His arguments were in vain. Apparently, Kluge's concern over Orsha decided him against giving his consent. He thought that the 20th Panzer Division might be able to provide assistance to the

Fourth Army. After consulting with the OKH, Kluge telephoned at midnight to cancel the intended attack until further notice.

Concerns of the headquarters of the Third Panzer Army in view of the oncoming winter defensive battle (Map 1)

Given the course of events on the front up to this time, how did the headquarters of the panzer army envisage the conduct of the oncoming winter battle? This question had arisen more and more frequently over the preceding few days. On 15 October, we presented to the army group a supplement to our memorandum on the conduct of a winter battle. In it, we sought to reiterate our point of view, to renew our warnings, and to respond to the changed situation brought about by the capture of Nevel.

The enemy, stated this second memorandum, could have hardly anticipated such a rapid capture of Nevel, i.e. five hours after the attack had begun. He had certainly not felt strong enough to take immediate advantage of his success. But since the enemy had yet to encounter any effective countermeasures from the German side, he surely must have seen *the* great opportunity that now existed. He was clearly reinforcing his flank protection, was trying at all costs to get his hands on the vital railway line connecting Velikiye Luki and Nevel, and was presumably still seeking to expand his breakthrough area to the south.

The memorandum then continued as follows:

> If the objective of the enemy's winter offensive is to cut off Army Group North by advancing on Riga, he will have to secure the narrow pass at Polotsk. This means that, in addition to his offensive on the southern flank, he will have to thrust towards Dünaburg via Vitebsk and Polotsk, or at least arrange an attack by the Rossono bandits. In this way, he will take the essential railway junction in Polotsk and thereby paralyse the flank of the Third Panzer Army. Vitebsk, as a major transportation hub, will always be a tempting target. The enemy has now reached a point 30 kilometres away from this city. Even in winter terrain, he will be able to carry out a frontal attack on Vitebsk between the Smolensk–Vitebsk railway and the Western Dvina; he will also be capable of approaching it from the south or along the north bank of the Western Dvina.

Our weak forces will be unable to repel a well-prepared and powerful Soviet offensive against the Panther Line, especially in the northern sector of the panzer army. The reserves at our disposal are insufficient. The ensuing consequences must now be dutifully pointed out. The high command of the Third Panzer Army is of the view that a hostile winter operation will unfold not only from the Nevel breakthrough area but also from the bandit territories of Lepel and Rossono. The extent of this operation and its impact upon Army Groups Centre and North cannot yet be foreseen. It may be crucial for the entire Eastern Front.

The number of personnel in the Third Panzer Army reached its lowest level in these critical days. While at the beginning of May there had still been 292,000 men, by 6 October there were only 200,000. In the meantime, the front of the panzer army had been extended by about 100 kilometres.

Renewed fighting in the Nevel breakthrough area (Map 3)

Until 16 October, the enemy remained relatively quiet along the front of the Nevel breakthrough area. There were significant changes in the depth of this area, especially north of the sector between Lobok and Lake Ordovo. The enemy appeared to be regrouping his forces, positioning replacements and new units, and equipping them all with fresh ammunition. A resumption of enemy attacks could be expected from this point onwards. How promising an attack of our own would have been during this regrouping! But Reinhardt's many requests on 15 October for authorisation to attack were denied by Kluge. Then a deserter brought news on 16 October of an imminent attack against the IX Corps. Even now, Kluge refused to give his approval to pre-empt this attack, although he did eventually admit that the IX Corps would need to go over to the defensive at once.

Our troops were therefore prepared to meet the Soviet attack, which commenced on the morning of 17 October. However, the enemy attacked with such force that after only a short time he had advanced well to the southwest of Lake Sadrach. He was partially brought to a halt by elements of the 20th Panzer Division, the 505th Tiger Battalion, and the reserves of the 129th Infantry Division. At the headquarters of the panzer army, we could not help thinking how much better everything would be going had we attacked on 16 October, when the enemy was still in the midst of preparations. Now the 20th Panzer Division was tied down under much less favourable conditions. On 18 October, it managed to regain the ground that had been lost on 17 October. The enemy suffered heavy losses, but our own ranks were so thinned out that a panzer-grenadier regiment of the 20th Panzer Division could no longer be withdrawn from the front. Relief forces were lacking.

CHAPTER 4

The retreat of the VI Corps to the Panther Line

On the right wing of the Third Panzer Army, the anticipated attacks from Rudnya had been launched on 6 October. Fierce fighting took place over the next few days. The withdrawal of the VI Corps was made particularly difficult by dense woodland, which the Soviets skilfully exploited by pursuing us rapidly. The enemy utilised a large number of tanks, and by 9 October we had put 95 of them out of action. Our troops, who had been fighting day and night for more than three weeks, were barely given a moment's respite to establish themselves behind a new line of defence.

Nonetheless, on 10 October we managed to withdraw behind the Panther Line, which had in the meantime been improved by all available staff and rear services. In an order of the day on 19 September, Reinhardt had appealed to all non-combatant units:

> In these decisive hours, where everything depends on giving the hard-fighting troops a well-prepared final position, I turn to all those elements of the panzer army not on the frontline to show true comradeship by setting to work immediately on the construction of this position. For the next two weeks, I expect all staff and units − officers and officials in the same way as non-commissioned officers and enlisted men − to put aside other tasks, to roll up their sleeves, and to strive to outdo one another. I request from all rear units a spirit of sacrifice for our fighters in the trenches.

This urgent appeal was most successful. Every unit sent every available officer, non-commissioned officer, and man to work day and night on the expansion of the Panther Line.

Despite his employment of seventeen guards and rifle divisions, four rifle brigades, three tank regiments, two mechanised brigades, and two antitank brigades, the enemy had been unable to penetrate the withdrawal front of the VI Corps. It now had to be expected that the Soviets would try, first, to bring about the collapse of the Panther Line before the commencement of the mud season, and second, to take Vitebsk. The focal point of the enemy attack was likely to be directed against the VI Corps and against the left wing of the LIII Corps. The latter, under General of the Infantry Friedrich Gollwitzer, had taken control of the right wing of the VI Corps (the 246th and 256th Infantry Divisions) upon entering the Panther Line.

Since 16 September, the troops had become accustomed to retreating on a daily basis. Reinhardt emphasised to them in an order on the day on 5 October that the Panther Line would be a strong winter defensive position:

> The panzer army has been involved in heavy defensive fighting for the last few weeks, and our adjacent armies have been so for months. By ceding ground to the enemy, we are now in a position to fight back and to inflict upon him losses that will far outweigh our own. The main objective of this fighting, to shorten the front and thus economise on the use of German forces, has been achieved.
>
> We shall henceforth hold this new position. I expect every single man to be as brave as he had been during the withdrawal. This position is to be defended to the last. No ground shall be yielded. Any piece of land that is lost must be retaken immediately.
>
> We all need to be imbued with the spirit of victorious defence, and must mercilessly obliterate any attack by the enemy on our new position. The best weapon is the fighting spirit. It is this that should drive every effort to bring the enemy advance to a standstill.

The enemy, under heavy bombardment, drew near to the Panther Line on 11 October. During our withdrawal, he had brought his battered units up to full strength with troops from replacement training regiments and with civilians, briefly trained (if at all), from recaptured territory. He brought forward further reinforcements and, as soon as 14 October, attempted to penetrate the Panther Line to the north of the Vitebsk–Smolensk road in order to maintain mobility and reach his first objective, Vitebsk. The Soviets were repelled along the entire front. In an almost uninterrupted series of assaults executed by ground-attack aircraft, tanks, and heavy artillery over the course of the next few days, the enemy sought to break through the new front to the west of Dobromysli and on either side of the Vitebsk–Liozno road and railway. Our infantry, whose combat strength had dropped severely, fought hard and kept the enemy at bay.

CHAPTER 5

Concerns about personnel

The bow was now stretched to breaking point. All of our warnings and all of our requests for reinforcements fell on deaf ears. On 18 October, we once more reported to Field-Marshal von Kluge at the command post of the army group, relating our anxiety about the serious shortage of manpower and about the gap between Army Groups Centre and North.

On our proposal to have the OKH deal with the boundary between the two army groups once and for all, Kluge replied: 'Oh, those people have little influence now. I have a feeling that Zeitzler will be leaving soon. He can no longer cope with the Führer. The two of them just shout at one another. Zeitzler's been exhausted for some time now. I hope he'll be replaced by Manstein.'

Regarding the alarmingly low – and continually decreasing – combat strength of the panzer army, Kluge said: 'I'm aware of the danger, and have written to the Führer. He might kick me out now, but in any case I can't do anything to help.' Kluge had written to Hitler on 14 October as follows:

> More and more of our divisions are in a state of deterioration. Replacements are lacking, and it is clear that too great a strain is being imposed on our troops. Never before has an army had such a high degree of mental and physical capacity demanded from it as in this war. I do not mean to suggest that morale is low. On the contrary, spirits are on the whole quite high, and it is, as ever, a great pleasure to speak to the men at the front. There is no bad sentiment to be spoken of.
>
> Nevertheless, the emptiness of the front trenches is most concerning, and it is no wonder if each man feels lonely and abandoned in the face of a massive assault by Russian infantry.

The preparedness of our replacement troops to bear all the consequences of soldiership is worsening significantly, and so too is their training. In some cases, we have had men sent to us who had never fired a shot. The leaders of the army have been following these developments with increasing anxiety.

At observation posts in recent days, I have personally seen how the absence of munitions has prevented our artillery from striking the most worthwhile targets. All of this creates the impression that the army is being neglected.

The army in its entirety was overjoyed when you, my Führer, became the leader of our Fatherland. You will not want to permit the army to decrease in value for you — possibly in favour of the other branches of the armed forces — when there is still the possibility of assisting it.

As the oldest officer in the Eastern Army, I believe that I am obliged to turn to you with complete confidence.[1] My subordinate commanders agree with me when I say that the Eastern Army in its current composition will be unable to cope, despite its determination, with an enemy offensive, especially in winter. There is a shortage of leaders, weapons, munitions, and, above all, men. Army Group Centre alone needs another 200,000 men. Recent losses are so great that there has been an alarming decline in the combat strength of the most heavily attacked units. No commander, regardless of his skill, can lead without men, weapons, and reserves. Any claim that the Russians also have shortages is simply untrue. Wherever he strikes, the Russian possesses everything that we lack. In the absence of any reserves, no commander is capable of mastering the long-term situation in the east.

I am speaking quite frankly. Only the clear recognition of the impending danger can, and will, bring about a remedy at the last moment. It is only because of the urgency of the situation that I ask you, my Führer, to read this letter and realise that it is your oldest officer in the Eastern Army who is writing, governed by no thought other than that of the duty and responsibility he bears towards you.

So the panzer army would receive no assistance for the time being. Our existing reserves had already been drawn upon to replace the significant casualties suffered by the corps formations. On 21 October, Colonel-General Reinhardt ordered that any counterattacks his subordinate commanders wished to launch would require his approval. This was an unusual measure, born out of concern for the daily losses that had escalated since the enemy's breakthrough. It severely restricted the freedom of action of these commanders. It also added to Reinhardt's responsibilities.

---

[1] Translator's note: The Eastern Army refers to the German Army on the Eastern Front.

The front of the panzer army was calm over the course of the next few days, although it became apparent that a new attack was being prepared against the IX Corps and the right wing of the LIII Corps.

Conference between the commanders of Army Group Centre and of the Third Panzer Army (Maps 1, 2, and 3)

The preparations for a new attack by the enemy induced Reinhardt to go and see Kluge once again in order to convey to him our concerns and recommendations. On 23 October, a serious discussion took place between both commanders, accompanied by their chiefs of staff, at the headquarters of the army group in Orsha. Reinhardt described the position of the enemy in front of the right wing of the panzer army. He said that substantial movements on the Rudnya–Liozno road were indicative of a major enemy offensive on either side of this road. There did not seem to be any plan to attack the VI Corps and the II Luftwaffe Field Corps. In contrast, there were growing signs of an attack being organised against the IX Corps, especially with the concentration of heavy artillery in the area to the south and to the southeast of Lake Ezerishche. Enemy fighters and anti–aircraft guns prevented aerial reconnaissance in the Nevel breakthrough area, though continuous movements could be observed from Velikiye Luki.

Reinhardt said that his visit was prompted primarily by Kluge's order that the 20th Panzer Division be detached from the panzer army and made available to the army group. 'This is impracticable,' he said. 'I must express this most emphatically. A detachment of this division is only possible in a few days' time, and only if a simultaneous order is given for the withdrawal, as has been requested for some time, of the II Luftwaffe Field Corps from its current protruding position to the Panther Line.' Kluge agreed that both orders would have to be given concurrently. Reinhardt stated that the II Luftwaffe Field Corps could reach the Panther Line by the night of 27 October if prior warning was given, and in response Kluge ordered that the retreat commence on the night of 25/26 October. At least one of our concerns had thus been resolved.

Reinhardt then proposed that another division be allocated to the panzer army in the event of the transfer of the 20th Panzer Division, for he would otherwise be without standby and security units for the impending defensive fighting. The field-marshal responded by saying that there was nothing he could provide. He was keeping Colonel-General Zeitzler informed on a daily basis regarding the seriousness of the situation and the alarmingly low level of our combat strength. However, he added, he had the feeling that Zeitzler no longer had the ear of the Führer. The news he had received confirmed this. It seemed no one could approach the Führer with such matters.

Reinhardt reported that he could no longer hand over the II Luftwaffe Field Corps, as had been ordered by the air force: 'If this order is upheld from above, I'll simply refuse to follow it. It is *my* responsibility to ensure the position is held.' Kluge replied: 'I'll cover up for you in every respect. While we at the front are of one view, those above seem to be of another. I set out these concerns quite clearly in my letter to the Führer, but have so far received no response. The Führer has read it, but hasn't discussed it with Zeitzler. Zeitzler thinks that the letter is very much on the Führer's mind. I don't know what will happen. Perhaps, by tomorrow, I'll no longer be sitting here on this chair.'

CHAPTER 6

Enemy activity in the Nevel breakthrough area from 18 October 1943

Enemy activity in the Nevel breakthrough area from 18 October was essentially characterised by:

- the conspicuous build-up of forces along the railway leading to Velikiye Luki from the east;
- the dispatch of new units from Velikiye Luki to the breakthrough area;
- the arrival of reinforcements to the east and southeast of Lake Ezerishche from the direction of Usvyaty, with the likely aim of bringing about the collapse of the northern cornerstone of the Third Panzer Army by enveloping it from the north and east;
- and finally, the initially hesitant probing on either side of Lake Ordovo, which was intended to create the conditions for outflanking our northern wing, for striking deep into the flank of the IX Corps, and for advancing along the railway towards Polotsk.

Underlining the operational intentions of the enemy were his constant reinforcement of fighter and anti-aircraft defences, the appearance of an Operations Staff 'North' of the air troops of the Red Army 35 kilometres northeast of Velikiye Luki, and his transfer of part of the staff of the Kalinin Front to the area northeast of Lake Ezerishche.

The Soviet advance from the Nevel breakthrough area (Map 4)

On 25 October, Kluge and Reinhardt once again spoke over the telephone. The former expressed his concern about Orsha and the boundary with the Fourth Army, but the latter replied that he was more worried about the left wing of the panzer army and its loss of contact with Army Group North. The high command of the panzer army re-emphasised its estimate of the situation in a report to Army Group Centre on 27 October. It was our opinion that the build-up in the Nevel area represented a great danger not only to the Third Panzer Army, but also to Army Groups North and Centre. This danger was abruptly illuminated on the next day when the enemy commenced his attack on our boundary with the Sixteenth Army. He enveloped the right wing of the Sixteenth Army and thereby increased the gap between the two army groups. Kluge was badly injured in a car accident that very day, and on 29 October he was replaced by the current commander of the Sixteenth Army, Field-Marshal Ernst Busch.

The 20th Panzer Division, with the exception of a few elements that were still in action, was dispatched to our right-wing neighbour, the Fourth Army, on 26 October. This further weakened the left wing of the panzer army. On the night of 27 October, the II Luftwaffe Field Corps was able to withdraw to the Panther Line according to plan and without enemy pressure.

On 29 October, the Soviets began to advance with three rifle divisions in the area to the west of Lake Ordovo. Faced with this development, Busch ordered that the 20th Panzer Division be returned to the Third Panzer Army and that the gap to the Sixteenth Army be narrowed with a counterattack. Before we could regroup for this counterattack, the enemy crushed two security battalions west of Lake Ordovo and pushed the Sixteenth Army further northwards. Consequently, the gap between the two army groups became so wide that the prospects of a successful counterattack, which had been planned for 3 November, were at an end, especially as the Sixteenth Army could not, and did not want to, participate in it. On 2 November, the army group, still seeking to re-establish contact with the Sixteenth Army, approved the cancellation of the northwestward attack from the Lake Ordovo area in favour of a northward attack from the Lobok area.

Three enemy groups lunged forward in the following days towards the south, the southwest, and the northwest:

- The first group, with one to three divisions, advanced southwards along the western side of Lakes Ordovo and Obol, reaching Zavan and the vicinity to its southeast on 9 November.
- The second group, with approximately two divisions, advanced southwestwards on either side of the Nevel–Polotsk railway line. By 7 November, the enemy had reached Dretun, and by 10–13 November he had been brought to a standstill by our police and security forces in the areas of Lake Meshno and Lake Chervyatka.
- The third group, with four divisions and two armoured units, advanced westwards and northwestwards, reaching the area to the south and to the southwest of Pustoshka on 10 November.

This three-pronged attack was launched with the utmost ferocity against our weakened, yet heroic, troops. It widened the gap that initially existed between Lakes Ordovo and Usvoya by about 14 kilometres, particularly to the north. The enemy outflanked the Third Panzer Army on one side and the Sixteenth Army on the other, after which he established contact with the bandits in the Rossono area. He also sought to break through the new front of the II Luftwaffe Field Corps, south and southeast of Lake Ezerishche, but he was driven off by our determined counterattacks.

Arrival of reinforcements for the Third Panzer Army

On 1 November, the panzer army had been promised reinforcements by the army group. Arriving in the Nevel breakthrough area by 6 November were the 252nd Infantry Division, two heavy antitank battalions (Tigers and Hornets), two assault-gun battalions, a heavy artillery battalion, a rocket projector regiment, and a motorised pioneer battalion.

By 4 November, the IX Corps had been supplied by the panzer army with the 87th Infantry Division (detached from the VI Corps), an assault-gun battalion, a heavy artillery battalion, and a rocket projector company.

The purpose of this concentration of forces, as decided on 2 November, was to attack northwards from the Lobok sector. The Sixteenth Army would advance southwards at the same time. Taking advantage of the lake-dotted land, our objective was to close the gap between Army Groups North and Centre and to cut off those enemy forces that had broken through to the west. This attack was planned for 8 November.

Anxious November days prior to the attack from the Lobok sector (Maps 4 and 5)

The daily progress of the Soviet thrust from the Nevel area towards the southwest, west, and northwest was alarming. The tension and crises during this time are illuminated by the following diary entries:

> **3 November:** Mist. The enemy attack from the Nevel area continues further to the southwest. We have nothing there to stop him. We had planned to send in the 252nd Infantry Division, but the army group has ordered it to the Lobok sector. As much as we welcome the attack from this sector, there is the danger that insufficient forces will be available for it.
>
> The enemy advance to the southwest remains almost unhindered. Combat near Klyastitsy. On our left, the enemy has advanced so far that we fear the Sixteenth Army will be out of position by 8 November.
>
> **4 November:** Clear and cold. Field-Marshal Busch is discussing our attack with the Führer. **10 am:** Conference at the headquarters of the panzer army. Preparations are in progress. The situation is most serious. Is a simultaneous offensive on Vitebsk from the east, on Gorodok from the northwest, and on Polotsk in the offing? There are several air strikes along the front. The enemy continues his unobstructed advance towards Dretun. Above all, he is in the process of encircling the Sixteenth Army.
>
> This evening, the decision has come from 'above' that we must finalise our preparations by 8 November. As much as we want to attack, might it be too late to do so by then?
>
> **5 November:** 10 degrees below zero. Colonel-General Reinhardt is with the 87th Infantry Division and the 20th Panzer Division. The 87th Infantry Division has relieved the 20th Panzer Division so that the latter will be available for the attack on 8 November.
>
> We repelled an enemy attack against the 6th Luftwaffe Field Division and 129th Infantry Division. There was also a minor attack against the 20th Panzer Division.

Our attack preparations are continuing, but so is the enemy advance. Southwest of Nevel, the enemy has reached the Dretun area. We have only weak security forces there, as if there is no enemy at all. Can we really get away with this?

6 November: Six degrees below zero. The outflanking by the enemy to the left of the 87th Infantry Division can only be insecurely covered. We must yield no ground, even though there are several points along the front where reserves and replacements are called for.

Conference with Field-Marshal Busch. He will help us as much as he can. Everything remains scarce. Even if our attack succeeds, he does not yet know how our weak forces can destroy the enemy divisions that have broken through. 'Cut off the enemy's retreat for a start, and then we may be in luck.'

In the evening, great concern over Polotsk. The army group will send some assistance.

In the evening, the army group reported to the OKH by telegraph its objectives for the attack of 8 November:

1. The Third Panzer Army shall attack with elements of the IX Corps from the Lobok sector and, with protection to the east and west, will take the land surrounded by Lakes Melkoye, Nevel, and Emenets.
2. The reinforced 252nd Infantry Division will break through the enemy position in the Lobok–Kurteleyevo sector and take the decisive high ground in Zui Shmotki. It will then drive on both sides of the main road to Lake Zaverezhye, fanning out along and holding the old Nevel defensive position (a line extending from one kilometre east of Zui Shmotki to Borok and to the southern tip of Lake Zaverezhye).
3. The reinforced 20th Panzer Division will break through the enemy position between Kosenkovo and Palkino, and will thrust through Ovinishche and Studenets towards Emenets. It is to reach the area between Lakes Melkoye and Nevel in the vicinity of Teleshovo, where it will create a blockade. Elements of the division shall also turn to the northwest and approach the Yemenka River between Lakes Nevel and Emenets. The further conduct of battle here will depend on the progress made by the Sixteenth Army in its own attack. Rear elements of the 20th Panzer Division are to swivel westwards and approach the Buslova-Shelu line, where they will cut off any enemy retreat between Lakes Emenets and Ordovo.

The diary entry for 7 November was as follows:

7 November: Snowfall. Great disappointment, for the Sixteenth Army wants to wait until 10 November before attacking. We alone are supposed to begin on 8 November. Our protest is of no avail.

We are most concerned about the situation on our left wing, where the envelopment of the 87th Infantry Division continues. We even have to mobilise military engineers for the defence.

The 129th Infantry Division reports that it is considerably worn out. It will have to rely on good fortune!

Final attempt to close the fatal gap between Army Groups Centre and North (Map 5)

After a heavy barrage on 8 November, the 252nd Infantry Division and the 20th Panzer Division commenced their attack from the Lobok sector. They advanced up to six kilometres, overcoming large minefields and taking a number of villages and high-ground locations. The fighting was tough, with heavy losses on both sides. There were some places where the enemy put up a particularly stubborn defence. In these battles, the 3rd Battalion of the 7th Grenadier Regiment acquitted itself with tremendous honour under the leadership of Captain Müller and, after he was seriously wounded, under the leadership of First Lieutenant Wiezens.

We had achieved a great deal, especially given the superior strength of the enemy. Our troops delayed the westward movement of strong Soviet forces by tying them down between Lakes Ordovo and Emenets. There was an improvement in morale everywhere, for we were finally moving forward again!

In the afternoon, the following message arrived at the headquarters of the panzer army: 'The OKH has issued the following order to Army Group North: From both sides of Nevel, it is the task of Army Group North to thrust to the west of Lake Nevel in order to reach the old boundary between the two army groups and thereby free up the forces of Army Group Centre that have pushed forward to the north of this line.'

With the plan of continuing our advance on 9 November in conjunction with the attack by the Sixteenth Army, we hoped that we might finally close the gap the next day. This would prevent further enemy forces from moving westwards, and would cut off supplies to those forces that had already broken through. We were fully prepared to proceed.

Officers and men alike were filled with anticipation. They were then to be bitterly disappointed by a telegraph message we received at 11:25 pm from the army group: 'Due to the development of the situation for the Sixteenth Army in the region to the northwest of Nevel, the intended attack by the I Corps cannot be carried out. The corps shall feign an attack by laying down heavy fire and conducting raids. The advance by the IX Corps is not to continue on 9 November. The corps must establish a favourable defensive line by holding the ground it has gained. A subsequent advance is possible.'

Would the sacrifices of the preceding days be in vain? There was no more time to lose if we wanted to continue our advance and foil Soviet plans! Reinhardt immediately telephoned Busch and, in a heated conversation, protested this order. He said that every postponement would make our eventual advance more difficult, for the enemy position was growing in strength every day. He then requested that the Führer make a final decision on this matter that very night. Busch agreed to this. Nevertheless, one of the regiments of the 211th Infantry Division, originally on its way to partake in the battle north of the Lobok sector on the next day, was kept in Vitebsk.

Hitler was in Munich for the commemoration of 9 November.[1] Because of this, his decision was delayed by more than an hour. This was enough to prevent the execution of the attack on 9 November in the way that we had intended. Then, at around 2:30 am, we received an OKH order that sought to outline how the gap between the two army groups could still be closed. It read:

> Having considered the situation in the Nevel combat zone, the Führer has decided that Army Group North must support the advance of Army Group Centre on the afternoon of 9 November or, at the latest, early on 10 November. Army Group Centre must at least push far enough on 9 November to be able to shut off the land routes between Lakes Ezerishche, Zaverezhye, Cherstno, Emenets, and Ordovo so as to prevent the enemy from systematically developing and strengthening his resistance.

---

[1]Translator's note: The Beer Hall Putsch was a failed attempt by Hitler to seize power on 8–9 November 1923. It was commemorated annually after he eventually took power in 1933.

Throughout 9 November, the enemy, as we had expected, attacked those elements of the IX Corps that had arrived the previous day. We repelled 21 attacks in fierce fighting, holding on to the territory we had gained. However, the IX Corps could no longer continue its advance. It was tied down by enemy assaults, and reinforcements had stopped arriving overnight.

CHAPTER 7

Commencement of the Soviet offensive east of Vitebsk

Despite the enemy's failure to penetrate the retreating frontline of the VI Corps, he had, from late October, been preparing to launch a major offensive on Vitebsk from the east. He had been steadily reinforced with rifle units, tank units, and artillery; he had been resupplied by road and rail; and he had been sizing up the strength of our front through numerous reconnaissance strikes. His preparations seemed to be substantially complete between 4 and 7 November. The increase in artillery bombardments, the frequency of aerial sorties, and the noise generated by tanks and motorised units all indicated that an enemy attack was imminent. Thus, the overall situation of the panzer army was characterised by the looming breakthrough from the east towards Vitebsk, and by the deep envelopment of the northern wing. There were no longer sufficient forces to resist a Soviet advance towards Gorodok or southwards towards the Polotsk—Vitebsk road near Sirotino.

In the late afternoon of 8 November, on the same day as our attack from the Lobok sector, the enemy began his advance against Vitebsk from the east with at least eight rifle divisions, one rifle brigade, two tank brigades, two mechanised brigades, and one tank regiment. He penetrated the central sector of the 206th Infantry Division, north of the Vitebsk–Liozno road, up to a depth of one kilometre and across a width of three kilometres. He also penetrated the front on the boundary of the 206th and 14th Infantry Divisions, south of Lake Vymno, to a depth of two or three kilometres and across a width of six kilometres. We were unable to deal with both points of penetration straightaway, and so in the evening twelve enemy tanks, accompanied by mounted infantry, charged several kilometres to the west.

Further diary entries illustrate the crisis–ridden days that followed:

> **9 November:** Mist. Air support is out of the question. Defence against multiple assaults. The situation is most serious for the VI Corps, with the enemy penetrating the front in two locations. We have a shortage of forces! The field-marshal renders assistance by sending the 211th Infantry Division as well as self-propelled assault guns, Hornets, and elements of the 211th Security Division. We shall extend the fronts of the LIII Corps and of the II Luftwaffe Field Corps in order to ease the strain on the VI Corps.

> **10 November:** Clear. We had made good progress with the advance on our northern wing, but in the afternoon we lost what we had gained. Our northern neighbour, the Sixteenth Army, achieved nothing at all, and now it is too late! What will happen? If we do not reach for one another, our efforts will have been in vain. We are already considerably overstrained. Three divisions are enveloped on the left.

> The VI Corps is involved in heavy fighting. The 211th Infantry Division will be very late, and so the enemy is continuing to make substantial inroads. The 206th Infantry Division is in an extremely difficult position. The IX Corps achieved all of its objectives this evening, which is a glimmer of hope! Tension with the field-marshal – he will not allow the 206th Infantry Division to retreat to the Bear Line. Unfortunately, only half measures have been ordered.

> **11 November:** Partially clear. The 206th Infantry Division has successfully disengaged. Even the heroic 301st Grenadier Regiment, which since 8 November has doggedly held its sector of the front on both sides of the points of penetration, is almost encircled and is withdrawing. Fierce combat in the area of the VI Corps is ebbing and flowing. A new frontline has largely been established, as ordered, although two gaps remain. There are enemy tanks behind this new front. They will have to go! We continue to lengthen the fronts of the neighbouring units so as to create new reserves for the VI Corps.

> The situation is becoming ever more serious in the deep flank of the IX Corps, so we will also have to send reserves there.

> **12 November:** Partially clear. Snow in the afternoon. The enemy tanks behind the 206th Infantry Division have come to a halt. The division has reduced the gap in its front. The enemy is less threatening than expected. His losses are considerable, thanks especially to our air force.

> **13 November:** Snow, thaw. All heavy attacks against the VI Corps have been repelled. Behind the right wing of the 206th Infantry Division are still several

thousand men with tanks. We can only maintain our guard against them, but our forces are really not enough.

14 November: Overcast, zero degrees. A somewhat quieter day. The enemy attack begins against the Fourth Army. The gap between the VI and LIII Corps, in the sector of the 206th Infantry Division, is still not closed.

15 November: Overcast, rain. There have been new, heavy assaults against the VI Corps, but everything is going well. A new guards division has arrived on the western flank of the IX Corps. The commander of the Third Panzer Army has warned the field-marshal that we are overstretched. Our neighbour on the left, the Sixteenth Army, needs to come quickly. It is nowhere near enough in reach.

16 November: Overcast. There has been fierce fighting and penetrations in the area of the VI Corps. With great difficulty, the commander of the panzer army has managed to withdraw the right wing of the corps. We have raised the alarm about the left flank, called for reserves, and requested that our left neighbour advance – all to no avail. **Afternoon crisis:** the breakthrough in the western flank by enemy cavalry and tanks poses a great danger to Gorodok and Sirotino, and obstructs two lines of supply!

CHAPTER 8

The critical development of the situation on the northern front, and withdrawal combat on the northeastern front

At 6:25 pm, Reinhardt reported the enemy breakthrough in the direction of Gorodok and Sirotino to Field-Marshal Busch. The Third Panzer Army did not want to stand idly by during an encirclement of the IX Corps. It was therefore necessary to immediately extricate the forces in the Lobok sector in order to create reserves for the Gorodok area. Busch rejected this possibility, refering to the Führer's order that the Lobok sector be held. Colonel-General Reinhardt replied as follows: 'Since the army group can spare nothing, and since the Lobok sector is to be held at all costs, we will have to economise on forces elsewhere. This will be possible northeast of Vitebsk by withdrawing the 14th Infantry Division from the salient, as along with the 4th, 3rd, and 6th Luftwaffe Field Divisions. I need to be granted the liberty to do whatever it takes to ensure the panzer army can hold out for a few days, at least until the advance by the Sixteenth Army from the north takes effect. I just want to be able to act, instead of having to look on.'

Busch said that the Führer would definitely refuse this proposal. He hoped for a decision the next day regarding the withdrawal from the Lobok sector. He concluded by saying: 'We are in this terrible struggle under a higher command that we have to obey, and which demands more than the utmost from our troops in the field.'

Nonetheless, the headquarters of the panzer army instructed the corps commanders to complete preparations for a withdrawal on the northeastern front on the night of 17/18 November, if possible without informing the field troops.

In a later discussion, Busch ruled out the proposed withdrawal of the northeastern front. If the Soviets took Gorodok, he said, there would be no alternative route of retreat. It would be best to keep calm and stand firm.

On this day, the II Luftwaffe Field Corps handed over its sector to the LIII Corps, which had in turn handed over its old area to the VI Corps on 14 November.

The crisis reached its peak on 17 November. In the afternoon of this cold, clear, winter day, a Soviet tank corps with three tank brigades and two or three rifle divisions was on the outskirts of Sirotino, pivoting towards Gorodok and Vitebsk. These forces were pushing forward along a 20-kilometre stretch of the front, and they were opposed only by the fragments of some construction battalions. Throughout the day, there were several heated telephone conversations between our commanders. They are reproduced here in part, so as to illustrate fully the challenging decisions that had to be made by the panzer army. At 12:20 pm, Reinhardt reported to Busch that strong Soviet tank forces were near Gorodok and Sirotino. He felt duty-bound to say that the current position could not be held and that an immediate decision on further operations was necessary.

> 'I am sorry to report that I cannot stand idly by and watch as the two corps are sacrificed.'
> 'That's not your decision. It's the Führer's.'
> 'Well, we need an immediate decision, but it has to suit our interests.'

Busch demanded that Gorodok be defended under all circumstances. Both of the corps there were not to be sacrificed by any means. He hoped that a decision would be made as early as lunchtime, when he would be attending a situation conference at the Führer's headquarters.

At 2:15 pm, Busch told us that the Führer had been informed and that he would make a decision after raising the matter with Army Group North at 3:30 pm. The Führer had already released a statement that was in accordance with the view of the panzer army. However, he had forbidden a withdrawal from the Lobok sector at this time, for it had yet to be decided when an attack would be launched by Army Group North. He had indicated that air supply could not be guaranteed in the event of parts of the panzer army becoming isolated. Reinhardt once more urged the need for a quick decision: 'I can't just sit back and watch an unfolding catastrophe. It's impossible. Someone else will have to take responsibility for this lack of action.'

At 6:25 pm, Busch informed us that Hitler would only make his decision at approximately 9 pm. The Führer wanted to speak first with the commander of Army Group North, Field-Marshal Georg von Küchler, who was still on his way. The OKH, which had striven to support the solution we had proposed, asked whether it was possible for just a single division to hold the current frontline in the four-lake area north of the Lobok sector. Reinhardt answered in the negative. He saw it as only a partial solution. The IX Corps, with two of its divisions in the lake area, was already fighting hard against enemy advances. We wanted to pull out both divisions and, as before, have the Lobok sector occupied by only a few battalions. The 20th Panzer Division would prevent the Soviets from taking Gorodok. It would also force its way along the Sirotino–Gorodok road. The 252nd Infantry Division would attack towards the southwest between Lakes Chernovo and Kosho.

Reinhardt's intentions would be telexed to the corps headquarters as a preliminary order at about 8:15 pm. However, the retreat from the Lobok sector would only commence when the final order was given at some point that night.

At 10:30 pm, Busch told us that one of the assault-gun battalions coming from the Reich, with approximately 40 assault guns, would arrive at Polotsk during the night. Meanwhile, the Führer had made his decision. He demanded that the 20th Panzer Division defend the present position in the Lobok bridgehead.

'Impossible', said Reinhardt.

'That remains to be seen', responded Busch.

'I can't guarantee a successful defence.'

'Neither of us can make such a guarantee, but we can be pleased that you've been given a certain freedom of movement.'

'It's a half measure.'

'It's not up for discussion.'

'Has a date been set for the attack by the Sixteenth Army?'

'I don't know. The Führer's current decision suggests that he's resolutely sticking to it as the sole way of clearing up the entire situation. We'd otherwise be putting our fate into the hands of the enemy. Once you start to make ground, you'll no longer have cause for concern.'

'I can make no guarantees.'

'No one's asking for guarantees. It's simply an order by the Führer. I can't do anything about it. I'm under the command of the Führer, and you are too. We must obey him. Be confident that things will look different tomorrow.'

Subsequently, the commander of the IX Corps, General of the Infantry Erich-Heinrich Clößner, declared that he did not think this order could be carried out, for the troops had already been made ready to retreat. Reinhardt reported this to Busch at about 10:45 pm. Busch then pointed out the difficulties to the OKH, but after half an hour he told us that the order would remain unaltered. The Führer attached great importance to maintaining the current position in the Lobok bridgehead.

It was difficult to have to watch everything unfold in exactly the way we had foreseen and reported for months. The situation need not have come to a head had any attention been paid to the warnings given by the headquarters of the panzer army. But instead, it was as if all hell was breaking loose across the entire Eastern Front. Reinhardt had never been so apprehensive as he was on this day. The development of the situation gnawed at him terribly. We would need a great deal of luck in the following days if we were to gain the upper hand.

CHAPTER 9

Further developments on the front to the east of Vitebsk

The enemy had launched a major offensive against the right wing of the VI Corps on 8 November. In fierce fighting on the following day, he managed to prise open the points of penetration. From the southern breakthrough area, in the vicinity of the 206th Infantry Division, he drove along the Vitebsk–Liozno road; from the northern, near the 14th Infantry Division, he advanced beyond Poddubye. Over the course of the next couple of days, additional Soviet forces attempted to expand the points of penetration and to crush from behind those German forces standing in between. The enemy had committed two new divisions, and he now pushed westwards through a gap which we had left to the south of the Vitebsk–Liozno road. On 12 and 13 November, the Soviets continued their relentless offensive, especially to the north and south of this road and to the west of Lake Vymno. Nevertheless, our last reserves held their position. The enemy's attacks abated after 17 November, presumably as a result of the considerable casualties he sustained. Rather than the intended breakthrough, the enemy had achieved little more than a local indentation in the frontline between the Vitebsk–Liozno railway and Lake Vymno. Through the brave conduct of two-and-a-half German divisions (half of the 246th Infantry Division alongside the 206th and 14th Infantry Divisions), the enemy had lost a guards rifle corps with four guards rifle divisions; two rifle corps with nine rifle divisions and two brigades; and a mechanised corps with two mechanised brigades, two tank brigades, and three tank regiments. Due to the development of the situation northwest and west of Gorodok, between 18 and 24 November the enemy sought to wear down our troops by constantly striking the front to the east of Vitebsk. He did so with forces ranging from company to regimental strength. Furthermore, the non-stop arrival of new forces to the battlefield east of Vitebsk demonstrated that the Soviets, despite their heavy losses, had not yet given up their intention of a frontal assault, presumably to be conducted simultaneously with an attack from the northwest.

CHAPTER 10

Combat and preparations for withdrawal on the northern front of the Third Panzer Army

In the Nevel combat zone, our troops had been blocking the enemy's route between Lakes Ordovo and Emenets since 10 November. We observed large formations moving westwards to the north of Lake Emenets, and bombarded them with our artillery. On 14 and 15 November, the Soviets, supported by tanks, repeatedly assaulted the Lobok bridgehead with five rifle divisions and one mortar brigade. Our counterattacks drove them back, and they suffered severe casualties in the process. It was clear that the intention of the enemy was to reopen the blocked route for further forces and supplies.

Between 8 and 15 November, a guards rifle corps, a guards division, a rifle division, and a mortar brigade had thrust deep into the breakthrough area south of Nevel. On 16 November, the Soviets renewed their attack and pierced the far western flank of the IX Corps, creating a gap approximately 15 kilometres in width. These rifle formations, accompanied by the recently arrived 5th Tank Corps, pushed towards the southeast and the south against fierce resistance. Thanks to a series of powerful counterattacks, we brought the enemy to a standstill along a line extending from Lake Bernovo to Lake Chernovo, Lake Kosho, west of Gorodok, west of Lake Losvida, and to the north of Sirotino.

It seemed that the Soviets had abandoned their offensive intentions against the southern wing of the Sixteenth Army in favour of strengthening their forces in the vicinity southeast of Lake Ezerishche and in the breakthrough area southwest of Nevel. In addition to those forces that had already come from the front facing the 16th Army, the enemy withdrew, one after another, four more rifle divisions and his Sixteenth Army, which he renamed the 11th Guards Army, as well as army artillery and mortar regiments from the area between Novosokolniki and Nevel.

The units following the enemy spearheads struggled to catch up. Supply was difficult, most of his artillery remained behind, and the mud season was developing rapidly. Enemy operations were more or less brought to a halt. The enemy even had to give up several villages west and southwest of Gorodok, where the 20th Panzer Division had been located since 19 November, when confronted with our counterattacks. We had only a weak obstacle-construction unit guarding the front between Lake Losvida and Sirotino. Security troops and police units held the front further to the west. The enemy, however, constantly sent new units into the breakthrough area, including two rifle divisions and the 3rd Guards Cavalry Corps. He thus indicated his intention of continuing offensive operations, just as in the sector of the VI Corps.

In the days following 17 November, the tension and crises on the northern wing of the panzer army grew from hour to hour. The combat strength of the IX Corps was sinking at an alarming rate. Even so, the enemy was holding back until he had moved his artillery, and probably also a tank corps, into position.

All the preparations by the panzer army for closing the gap at Nevel would be useless if we ended up being compelled to act under pressure from the enemy. Besides, we were simply too weak. This time, we would have to act quickly to avoid being too late.

Knowing that Field-Marshal Busch planned to meet with Hitler the following day, Reinhardt reported to the chief of staff of Army Group Centre, Lieutenant-General Hans Krebs, to point out once more the extreme danger to the northern wing of the panzer army. He said that although the enemy had yet to mount his offensive, our weakened forces were already unable to defend the northern and Gorodok sectors simultaneously. Only one or the other could be adequately reinforced. If the Lobok bridgehead had to be held, further reinforcements would be necessary. Otherwise, continued Reinhardt, on the next day the Führer would surely be compelled to approve a rapid withdrawal of the northern wing of the panzer army. The tension was growing by the hour. The enemy was applying considerable pressure in the Lobok sector and against the LIII Corps. The combat strength of the 20th Panzer Division and the 252nd Infantry Division had deteriorated considerably. They were now of regimental size, capable of conducting local raids, but no longer able to effect a turnaround. The corps headquarters had already been ordered on 20 November to prepare for the possible withdrawal of the northern front. The army group would be informed of these preparations. The field-marshal, concluded Reinhardt, would need to make clear to the Führer that it had become too late to go on the offensive.

In the evening, a message arrived from the headquarters of the Sixteenth Army. It outlined a plan of attack that would begin on 22 November. It would take place to the southwest of Pustoshka with the aim of annihilating the enemy forces in the northwest part of the breakthrough area. The gap between Lake Lovets and the eastern end of Lake Yazno would foreseeably be closed by 29 November, and only thereafter would the lake-dotted region around and to the south of Nevel be retaken.

'I can't work with this timeframe', said Reinhardt when he met with Busch at 9:15 pm. 'If we're to close the gap at Nevel, the panzer army must be reinforced immediately. Otherwise, the entire operation will collapse. The decision on the future conduct of operations depends heavily on us making every effort in the present situation.' Busch agreed with this appraisal of the situation. He was to meet with Hitler the next day, and promised to speak in favour of Reinhardt's proposal.

On 22 November at 4:55 pm, whilst the details of a large-scale withdrawal were being discussed with the corps commanders (none of whom doubted that it would commence that evening), Reinhardt received from Krebs the decision of the Führer. It had been made after the meeting with Busch, and its content was quite unexpected: 'The

Third Panzer Army shall hold its current position. It is important to push the enemy back from the road that runs through Gorodok. By closely coordinating all available construction forces, new switch positions are to be built as quickly as possible from Lake Kosho in a straight line to the east and on both sides of Lake Losvida.'

Shortly afterwards, we learnt from Busch that the advance of the Sixteenth Army was progressing well. The Führer had indicated that its success, despite the inferiority of its forces, was due to the fact that the Soviets had not been resupplied for several days. It was for this reason that he had ordered the Third Panzer Army to remain in its current position. The Führer was convinced that any further enemy action from the vast breakthrough area would be insignificant.

We were just as horrified at Hitler's decision as we were at his view that there would be little more enemy activity in the breakthrough area, for there were in fact an overwhelming number of hostile troops there. But time was pressing, and the corps commanders were awaiting the decision. With a heavy heart, Reinhardt decided to inform the commanding generals about the Führer's order and to cancel all preparations for the retreat of the northern front.

Only good fortune could now help the two corps and their brave troops, who had already performed superhuman feats in the last few weeks. At around 11 pm, Reinhardt issued an order of the day, which was announced to all the troops in the shortest possible time:

> This afternoon, the Führer called on all of us to hold our positions until the last moment in order to lay the groundwork for the destruction of the enemy forces that have penetrated the front near and to the southwest of Nevel. The most severe period is now behind us. Nonetheless, it is now necessary to hold out in this grave, decisive hour. I am relying upon every single one of you. We must, and will, do what the Führer expects of us. This is about Germany! We have faith in, and our lives belong to, the Fatherland.

And fate was truly kind to us. According to some intercepted radio messages, the Soviets were going to be ready by 25 November to strike our northern wing from the east, north, and west. But, surprisingly, a thaw set in on 24 November. Roads were transformed into mud in no time. All large-scale movements were neutralised. Consequently, the Soviets were plagued by supply difficulties. Their attack had to be cancelled.

It was thanks to the mud that the daily reports of the panzer army over the course of the next three weeks began with: 'No major engagements', 'The enemy continues to remain quiet', 'No infantry activity along the entire front of the panzer army', or 'Preparations by the enemy for an attack against the northern wing have been checked'.

CHAPTER II

Suspected enemy intentions after the frost returned

Despite, or perhaps precisely because of, this period of calm before the impending onslaught, Reinhardt again requested authorisation to withdraw the northern wing of the Third Panzer Army before the frost returned. Field-Marshal Busch shared our view. Even Colonel-General Kurt Zeitzler spoke twice with the Führer about the need for a decision in favour of the proposal put forward by the panzer army. Hitler rejected it.

In which sectors, with what objectives, and at what time would the Soviets commence their major offensive against the panzer army – whose front was now 300 kilometres in length – in order to dislodge our troops from Vitebsk?

It was becoming apparent from recent combat operations that the enemy sought at all costs to establish a favourable starting position for an offensive in the direction of the Baltic states before the onset of winter. This starting position would have to be in the area of Nevel–Novosokolniki–Pustoshka or of Vitebsk–Nevel. Therefore, either the southern wing of Army Group North or the northern wing of the Third Panzer Army would have to be brought to its knees. Either scenario was possible given the current concentration of Soviet troops. In any case, the large number of Rossono bandits would be useful for the enemy. They were prepared to make contact with the Red Army, and would allow the bloodless occupation of an area that would lead right up to the gates of Dünaburg.

The concentration of enemy troops before the boundary between Army Groups North and Centre was becoming increasingly evident through the arrival of new Soviet armies, the pinpoint bombing by formations of the Red Air Force, and the creation of a 'Baltic Front' (a Soviet army group).

The enemy hoped that Army Group Centre would crumble. After his breakthrough near Nevel, his rapid success against weak security troops west of Gorodok, and his victories against the two southern armies of Army Group Centre (the Ninth and Second Armies), he certainly seemed to be fixated on the elimination of the northern wing of the Third Panzer Army. To execute this, he transferred strong forces away from the southern wing of the Sixteenth Army and positioned them for the attack against our northern wing.

As the enemy prepared his attack, it became clear that he would apply his greatest effort at the following locations:

- east of Vitebsk between the Vitebsk–Smolensk railway and the Vitebsk–Surazh road;
- southeast of Lake Ezerishche;
- from Lake Chernovo to either side of Lake Bernovo;
- and in the breakthrough area to the west of Gorodok.

With his forces assembled in these locations, the enemy would attempt to bring about the collapse of the northern wing of the panzer army by launching a simultaneous attack from the east towards Vitebsk, from the northeast and southwest towards Bychykha, and from the depth of the breakthrough area towards Gorodok or towards the traffic hub of Polotsk. The strength of Soviet infantry in the area would determine whether Gorodok or Polotsk would be the target. At this stage, it seemed that he lacked sufficient infantry for an ambitious offensive. However, he could have planned a surprise assault on Polotsk had he spotted our weak forces to the northeast of the city. That said, the two rifle divisions that had hitherto stood opposite the Lobok sector had yet to reappear.

The delay in the enemy's attack preparations could undoubtedly be attributed to the spell of bad weather and the associated impassibility of his roadways. For the same reason, only about half of his potential divisional artillery could be present in the breakthrough area to the southwest of Nevel. Moreover, the enemy had to expend as little ammunition as possible. But it could be expected that, after the onset of the first long period of frost, the enemy would make every effort to stockpile supplies and to top up on fuel, so as to ensure the longevity of his offensive operations. Once the enemy was underway again, we could presume that he would have already consolidated his routes of supply.

CHAPTER 12

The first winter defensive battle around Vitebsk

With a slight frost setting in on 9 December, the roads could be used again. The enemy immediately hastened his preparations for the offensive. This was indicated by numerous holding attacks, by scouting raids, by adjustment artillery fire, and by the extensive movement of enemy troops and supplies behind those sectors of the front where the offensive was anticipated.[1] The enemy could now strike at any time. The army group once more ordered that the troops hold their current position. Under no circumstances would local penetrations by the enemy be permitted to give rise to a retreat.

The first crisis-ridden days of fighting on the northern front of the panzer army, and our efforts to enable its retreat (Map 8)

On 13 December, the Soviets began their major pincer attack against the northern wing of the Third Panzer Army. The first winter defensive battle around Vitebsk, which would last 37 days, had commenced.

---

[1]Translator's note: A holding attack involves pinning down the enemy in a particular position whilst conducting a main attack elsewhere. Adjustment artillery fire involves placing fire on or near a target, and, guided by an observer, making adjustments as necessary to improve accuracy.

Four rifle divisions and approximately 45 tanks attacked from the northeast to the south of Lake Ezerishche, where the 129th Infantry Division was located. At the same time, two rifle divisions and approximately 50 tanks advanced from the southwest against the 20th Panzer Division, between Lakes Bernovo and Chernovo. The right wing of the 129th Infantry Division, four kilometres in width, was pushed back. In the evening, the enemy reached the Nevel–Gorodok road, and we had to employ our last reserves to stop him there. The enemy also managed to push back the 20th Panzer Division by three kilometres, but even here he had to pause after our counterattacks contributed to the destruction of 27 of his tanks.

On the evening of 13 December, Field-Marshal Busch responded by telex to our assessment of the situation, in which we continued to advocate a timely withdrawal of the northern wing of the panzer army. Busch stated that such considerations would be unambiguously rejected. As ever, the Führer saw the annihilation of enemy forces in the vicinity west of Nevel as the ultimate goal, the precondition of which was that the panzer army maintain its current position. Busch was convinced that the troops of the Third Panzer Army could stand firm and that they would thereafter be instrumental in destroying the enemy formations west of Nevel. The forces required for a coordinated operation with the Sixteenth Army would then be made available for this purpose.

On 14 December, the 129th Infantry Division defended its position twice against barrage fire, each lasting two hours. The enemy failed to make any significant territorial gain. However, he penetrated the front by up to two kilometres in the middle sector of the 87th Infantry Division, where a lone military construction company was to be found. This penetration could only be blocked by drawing upon forces elsewhere, thereby weakening the rest of the front. The enemy broke through the defensive front of the 20th Panzer Division at several points and advanced right up to the railway to the west of the Nevel–Gorodok road.

Reinhardt visited the front of the IX Corps in the morning. The corps had been under the command of Lieutenant-General Rolf Wuthmann since 8 December. Reinhardt, seeing for himself the way in which events were unfolding, telephoned Busch and requested that the 129th and 87th Infantry Divisions withdraw to a line connecting Khvoshko, Askerino, and Lake Bernovo. The field-marshal then explicitly pointed to his telex message from the day before. He said that the request for a retreat, which seemed to have originated with the IX Corps, would not be approved by the Führer. The panzer army was to ensure that the situation develop in the manner as had been outlined the previous day.

At 1:30 pm, the IX Corps renewed its request. It did so again 25 minutes later, as the enemy had gained more ground to the northeast of Lake Bernovo. There was a growing danger that the two northern divisions might be encircled. Reinhardt, who in the meantime had returned to the headquarters of the panzer army, immediately informed Busch of the deteriorating situation, which had become most critical as a result of the penetration of the front of the 87th Infantry Division. Busch once more stressed the need for standing firm. However, all he transferred from the army group reserve to the IX Corps was the rein-forced regimental group of the 197th Infantry Division. It would not arrive until noon the next day.

In the first few hours of the night of 14/15 December, the enemy pushed further westwards against the 129th Infantry Division. We had only radio contact with those troops that remained in the Lobok sector. The situation worsened by the hour. At 2:15 am, the IX Corps asked that these northernmost troops be allowed to withdraw. Shortly there-after, Wuthmann drew Reinhardt's attention to the fact that it would soon be impossible to supply the two divisions. At 3:20 am, Wuthmann reported to Reinhardt that the regimental commander in the Lobok sector had asked over the radio for permission to disengage, as it was likely that the position would be untenable later that day. Reinhardt was compelled to deny such permission. If this regimental group were to fall back, it would completely expose the flanks and rear of the 129th Infantry Division. He ordered that the utmost be done to hold the front in the north. Should this front be forced back by the enemy, then it should withdraw no further than the Obol River.

In the early morning of 15 December, the situation continued to deteriorate across the entire sector of the 129th and 87th Infantry Divisions. Strong enemy forces flowed into the uncontrollable gap that had opened up in the west of the 129th Infantry Division. We were unable to ascertain which enemy units made up this tide. At 8 am, the enemy spearheads from the east and west were only 10 kilometres away from one another. In the course of that morning, the Soviet forces that had broken through the front of the 129th Infantry Division struck the rear of the defenders of the Lobok sector. Furthermore, the penetration point in the front of the 87th Infantry Division was expanded eastwards and northeastwards by the 26th Guards Division. The northern part of the 87th Infantry Division therefore had to be withdrawn. The danger of two pockets being formed grew ever greater. Nevertheless, Reinhardt once again felt obliged to reject an immediate retreat by the IX Corps, for it would be too hazardous to execute by day. He said that towards noon, when Busch would be arriving at the headquarters of the panzer army, it might be possible to make a decision for the evening.

Enemy tanks east of Lake Bernovo made a breakthrough to the northeast. The high command of the panzer army could no longer intervene helpfully in the rapidly crumbling situation. Every man now had to fight where he stood. We had to wait until Busch, departing Minsk by plane at 11:30 am, arrived at the headquarters of the panzer army before new decisions could be made. Upon his arrival, he was immediately informed by Reinhardt of the further worsening of the situation. With the available forces, argued Reinhardt, an encirclement of the two northern divisions could not be prevented. He therefore proposed that the northern wing retreat to the line connecting Khvoshko, Askerino, and the northern end of Lake Bernovo as soon as the position and the time of day would allow. In a heated discussion with Busch, who repeatedly pointed to the Führer's great solution, Reinhardt emphasised the necessity of his own proposal. The 87th Infantry Division, under attack from two sides, had been partially hurled back from its position. Consequently, the gap to the south of Nevel had been prised open so much that the conditions for a counterattack to close it, as the Führer had in mind, no longer existed.

At 12:20 pm, the field-marshal, now convinced by Reinhardt, recommended to the OKH that the IX Corps retreat immediately in accordance with the proposal of the Third Panzer Army. An hour later, he told Colonel-General Zeitzler that the last moment for a decision had come. It was time to extract the still combat-ready units, especially the artillery, from the impending encirclement.

Towards 2 pm, we received the approval of the Führer for the withdrawal of the northern wing. This was a great relief. We were finally free from the tremendous tension that had weighed heavily on everyone in the last few hours. Although the battalions in the Lobok sector and the 87th Infantry Division had by now been encircled, it was hoped that they would push southwards and punch through the ring of encirclement.

This first withdrawal had far-reaching consequences. It was quite clear to us at the headquarters of the Third Panzer Army that this disengagement would just be the first step. Our forces had to be freed as soon as possible so that they could establish a new, realigned defensive front to the west of Sirotino.

The encirclement of and the breakout by the 87th Infantry Division (Map 8)

On the evening of 15 December, the enemy spearheads were only a few kilometres away from one another. The enemy forces northeast of Lake Bernovo had advanced so far that the encirclement of the 87th Infantry Division and of the Lobok garrison had practically been completed. The 129th Infantry Division was ordered to retreat to the Khvoshko–Askerino line during the night. Whether the 87th Infantry Division could reach the line from Askerino to Lake Bernovo depended on its ability to repel the enemy forces that had encircled it. Otherwise, it was ordered to strike towards the southeast and to close the gap between Askerino and the right wing of the 20th Panzer Division. This latter division was positioned along the section of railway that ran from the northwest of Malashenki to the eastern tip of Lake Chernovo.

Several anxious hours passed by, during which we were uncertain about the fate of the 87th Infantry Division. Difficult terrain slowed its progress, and we lost radio contact early on 16 December. Nevertheless, we all hoped for a successful breakout. Reinhardt was at the front, and he warmly requested of the troops that they hold out longer so as to ease the struggle of the 87th Infantry Division.

The 129th Infantry Division had withdrawn overnight. It was still embroiled in fierce defensive combat in its new position, where it was under pressure from five enemy divisions with two tank brigades. These enemy forces also encountered the left wing of the 6th Luftwaffe Field Division. The enemy launched an assault from the west with the bulk of five divisions and strong elements of the 5th Tank Corps against the combat groups under the command of the 20th Panzer Division. Many ground-attack aircraft supported the enemy assault by keeping the main road under constant fire. Through determined defence and counterattack, we were able to hold the railway line. A three-kilometre gap opened up between the 129th Infantry Division and the 20th Panzer Division, through which the enemy attacked, and he reached the main road at a point five kilometres to the north of Malashenki.

Towards 4 pm, we received the good news that the 87th Infantry Division, together with the troops from the Lobok sector, had successfully broken free of the ring of encirclement. Even though without artillery, without heavy weapons, and with few vehicles, approximately 5,000 men had reached Malashenki whilst constantly fighting off two or three enemy divisions at temperatures as low as six degrees below zero. There was no news on the whereabouts of the rest of the 87th Infantry Division. The lead elements of the division (approximately 200 men) had overrun a Soviet battery upon approaching our main defensive line. The noise of battle had drawn enemy riflemen near. But these 200 men had rushed forward to the German lines with 'Deutschland, Deutschland, über alles' on their lips, thereby paving the way to freedom for their following comrades.

The most combat-effective division of the panzer army had been decimated. Some of its men had been saved, but all of its weapons and equipment had been destroyed! It was yet another 'too late' situation. The division would surely have escaped in a less weakened state had the order to withdraw, so urgently sought by the high command of the panzer army, been given 24 hours earlier. It would now be several days before the division could be used again. It needed to be re-equipped with heavy weapons, and its units had to be reorganised. The retreat of the division on this day had resulted in the loss (dead, wounded, and missing) of 45 officers, 1,496 non-commissioned officers and men, and 212 auxiliary volunteers. All artillery, heavy weapons, and vehicles, as well as nearly all horse-drawn vehicles, had been lost. They had become bogged down in the mud and, where the situation had allowed, had to be blown up and left behind.

Even now, those 'above' were not yet ready to draw the conclusions from recent events and to order the large-scale withdrawal that we had long sought, especially before further forces were crushed in this utterly pointless salient. Instead, the army group announced that front of the panzer army would be reinforced with two new divisions, including the Panzer-Grenadier Division Feldherrnhalle. However, only the first elements of both divisions arrived in the next few days.

There was an unpleasant telephone conversation between Reinhardt and Busch that night. Field-Marshal Busch took the colonel-general to task because the 87th Infantry Division had returned without artillery or heavy weapons. Regarding this telephone conversation, excerpts from a letter written by Reinhardt to Busch are reproduced below. Reinhardt sent this letter to Busch the next day, after he had spoken with the commanders in the 87th Infantry Division. It illuminated the difficulties encountered by the division during its withdrawal, but also bespoke the chivalry of the commander of the panzer army:

> Yesterday, I had to report that, although much of the 87th Infantry Division had succeeded in charging through the enemy forces, its heavy weapons and artillery had to be sacrificed in the process.
>
> This news had initially filled me with disappointment, all the more so because the division had made a name for itself under its previous commander, Lieutenant-General Walter Hartmann, who has recently been the recipient of the Oak Leaves to the Knight's Cross of the Iron Cross. Until recently, the division had been the only one in the panzer army that, according to an assessment of its combat effectiveness, could still 'carry out limited attacks'.
>
> Today, I have spoken with those commanders of the division who have returned. In particular, I spoke at length with the artillery commander, Major Rudolf Böckmann, a recipient of the Knight's Cross. I also had the divisional commander, Colonel Mauritz Freiherr von Strachwitz, relate to me the execution of the breakout.

I now provide a summary of my impressions:

The task of the 87th Infantry Division was especially difficult due to the strength of the enemy on all sides and to the marshland that characterised the terrain. The disengagement from the enemy and the retreat to the east over the Obol was carried out in the southern sector under strong enemy pressure and in the central sector relatively easily. All weapons and vehicles accompanied this initial retreat. In the northern sector, the retreat failed to go according to plan. If the troops and vehicles there, including those from the Lobok garrison, were to escape, they would have to force their way out via Laptevka. The resistance of the enemy was so strong here that he could not be thrown back, even though the energetic and brave regimental commander, Colonel Helmut Geißler, a recipient of the Knight's Cross, personally led the attack. He fell on the frontline. Some of the troops, including the battalions from the Lobok sector, managed to fight their way through at various points, but our vehicles could not advance through the marsh forest. As a result, the northern combat group, which had been earmarked to take over the defence of the left wing, effectively lost its opportunity for any further breakthrough, as it could no longer utilise its artillery and heavy vehicles.

Thus, the breakthrough of the bulk of the division was conducted on either side of the Maslyaki–Malashenki line. In addition to the considerably difficult terrain, the darkness meant that the assembled troops could not yet go into action. They would have to wait until morning to do so. Rolling stock had to be abandoned. Only heavy weapons, artillery, and light vehicles were kept moving for transporting the wounded. With the commencement of the breakthrough attack, the troops initially encountered little resistance from enemy infantry. However, he soon reinforced himself, and our troops came under heavy artillery fire. Along with the other commanders in the division, Colonel Freiherr von Strachwitz, who himself led the main group, declared that the grenadiers knocked down everything in their path. They broke through into the lines of enemy artillery and destroyed five batteries, thereby accomplishing the first critical stage.

The enemy then counterattacked. Tanks came at our troops from the left. Enemy fire necessitated a shift of the advance of the mass of the division into a well-covered streambed to the northwest of Malashenki. Our vehicles, vulnerable in the daylight, were also forced to enter this terrain. Several difficulties soon arose, which ultimately led to these vehicles getting stuck. Even the track-laying vehicles of the accompanying rocket projector battalion became bogged down. Despite all efforts in the somewhat frozen and uneven terrain, it was apparent that few horse-drawn vehicles would have been able to make it through. The vivid account given to me by the artillery commander of how our troops struggled forward and tried everything, to no avail, to salvage our vehicles can only be completely understood by those familiar with the pitfalls of the land in the east. It was under these circumstances that our vehicles and artillery pieces, and eventually also our rocket projectors, were destroyed. As far as possible, the horse-drawn units fought alongside the troops, carrying only small arms, through the last enemy barrier. Some light antitank guns and light vehicles carrying the wounded also made it to the end.

I regard it as my duty to stand up for the division. To reproach it for the loss of its heavy weapons and artillery, and to thereby question the reputation of a division that has proven itself in the last few months, is in my view unjustifiable.

I request that my view is made known to the leadership, for I fear that, after last night's telephone conversation, the OKH or the OKW would otherwise develop an incorrect perspective.

I feel obliged to write this message. It would be particularly painful for me as the commander if the reputation of the tried and tested 87th Infantry Division were to be unjustly damaged.

Further combat during the retreat of the northern front (Map 8)

On 17 December, the enemy, partly reinforced with fresh units, continued to apply strong pressure against the northern and northwestern fronts of the IX Corps. He made new inroads against the 129th Infantry Division, which lacked the forces necessary to hold its extended front. Of those parts of the 87th Infantry Division that had escaped from the encirclement, only two companies were ready for action. At noon, the high command of the panzer army recommended to the army group that the LIII and IX Corps withdraw that night to the line extending from the northern end of Lake Vymno to the eastern end of Lake Chernovo. Yet again, we had to wait several hours for a decision to be made. And yet again, it was only a half-measure that was decided upon, by which time it was approaching 4:15 pm. Reserves were unavailable, and another salient formed in the front. Only a retreat to the Maksimovka–Vyshedki–Malashenki line was permitted. The corps commanders were outraged! Reinhardt argued further with Busch over need for a large-scale withdrawal, but it was all in vain. The field-marshal ended the telephone conversation with these words: 'We're living from hand to mouth. Where there's fire, it must be put out with what meagre resources we have. I can offer the armies no assurances. I'm aware of the dangers, but can't do anything about them as long as I'm given nothing extra to command.'

In the evening, we received a telex message from the army group. In it, Busch elaborated on his rejection of our recommendation:

> The Führer has ordered: 'Field-Marshal Busch has the freedom to withdraw the divisions of the northern defensive line to a position between Lakes Vymno and Kosho. However, this is only to take place amidst fierce combat and by defending every square metre of ground. The aim is to inflict heavy losses on the enemy as he advances and to deny him the chance of launching an immediate offensive on Polotsk and to its east. Furthermore, we shall gain time so as to be able to enhance the defence of the northern wing.'
>
> To this end, I order: The situation of the 129th Infantry Division necessitates a limited, gradual, and fighting withdrawal of the 3rd Luftwaffe Field Division, the 6th Luftwaffe Field Division, and the 129th Infantry Division to the Maksimovka–Vyshedki–Malashenki line, which is then to be held. In fulfilling the Führer's order, it is important to keep the gap to the south of Nevel as narrow as possible for the enemy and to cause him the heaviest losses. The 3rd Luftwaffe Field Division is to halt its retreat once it reaches a point just to the northeast of Maksimovka.

On this day, the high command of the panzer army made the following report: 'Even after the disengagement of 17/18 December, there are insufficient infantry forces that can be brought together to support the western front of the IX Corps, against which further powerful attacks are expected. If the 6th Luftwaffe Field Division is to be given freedom of movement, both it and the 3rd Luftwaffe Field Division ought to be allowed to retreat to the line between Lake Vymno and Vyshedki. In view of the vulnerability of the western front, a rapid withdrawal of the 3rd Luftwaffe Field Division to the aforementioned line, and thereby the release of the 6th Luftwaffe Field Division, must be considered crucial for the conduct of operations in the coming days.'

Our night-time withdrawal was pursued by the Soviets, who applied particularly strong pressure against the 129th Infantry Division and on either side of the main road. Until the 6th Luftwaffe Field Division, under the command of the LIII Corps, penetrated the front on 19 December, we managed to repel several tank-supported attacks against our new position. There was further haggling with the army group at noon over new intermediate lines, which were simply another half-measure. This time, though, the decision taken was in our favour. It was thus that the 3rd Luftwaffe Field Division could be brought back to the Lake Vymno–Vyshedki line. Several attempts by the enemy to break through the northern and northwestern fronts on 19 December were repelled by the IX Corps. Finally, we were given authorisation to withdraw the northern front to the Shishkovo–Lake Chernovo line during the night of 19/20 December. The 6th Luftwaffe Field Division could therefore be pulled out and relocated to the area northwest of Lake Losvida.

The arrival of reinforcements, and the assumption of responsibility for the northern front by the LIII Corps (Map 7)

Arriving in the area of the panzer army from 18 December were:

- the 197th Infantry Division, which was in panzer army reserve and stationed to the northeast of Vitebsk until 24 December (although two of its regimental groups were already in use by the IX Corps);
- the Panzer-Grenadier Division Feldherrnhalle, which, not yet ready for action, was in army group reserve to the northwest of Vitebsk until 21 December; and
- the 5th Jäger Division, which until 26 December was assembled to the northeast of Polotsk.

From 18 December, the 87th Infantry Division was relocated by rail to the south of Ula for refitting and refreshing. At 8 am on 20 December, the LIII Corps assumed responsibility for the sector previously defended by the IX Corps, as ordered by Reinhardt:

> The battle on the northern wing of the Third Panzer Army has been ongoing since 13 December. However, the exceptional defence of the IX Corps has now succeeded against far superior enemy forces. One hundred and forty-two enemy tanks have been put out of action.
>
> The 20th Panzer Division has not only prevented a decisive breakthrough of the 4th Russian Shock Army (six reinforced rifle and guards rifle divisions and three tank brigades) along the Nevel–Vitebsk road, but has also caused the enemy considerable losses, especially in tanks. The divisional commander, Lieutenant-General Mortimer von Kessel, was wounded in the course of these battles.
>
> Particularly praiseworthy is the sacrificial commitment of the 87th Infantry Division in its fight on all sides against vastly superior enemy forces. The

division broke through enemy lines with unparalleled bravery, inflicted heavy casualties on enemy troops, and annihilated several tanks and more than eleven batteries.

The most powerful attacks were directed against the 129th Infantry Division which, just like the 6th Luftwaffe Field Division, played an outstanding role in the destruction of strong enemy forces. Fighting ceaselessly against the 11th Guards Army (eight reinforced rifle divisions and four tank brigades), the division intercepted and counterattacked the enemy thrust along the road to Gorodok. The enemy was weakened so much that success eluded him.

The winter defensive battle spreads to the front east of Vitebsk (Maps 6 and 7)

According to the news broadcasted on the radio in the Fatherland on 19 December: 'The heavy combat in the vicinity of Nevel makes the remaining battles on the Eastern Front pale in comparison.'

To the east of Vitebsk, only half an hour after this broadcast, a one-and-a-half-hour heavy barrage commenced against a 12-kilometre section of the right wing of the 14th Infantry Division. After that, the enemy launched a major offensive in this area, as we had been anticipating for the last few days. He attacked with eight rifle divisions, one rifle brigade, and two tank units. The land to the north and east of Vitebsk was now ablaze. The winter defensive battle had entered a new, intensified phase. Three days of the toughest defence began. To the east of Vitebsk alone, 124 enemy tanks were destroyed.

Preparations by the enemy for this offensive had already been apparent in the second half of November. Movements before the 256th, 246th, and 14th Infantry Divisions had been observed, and from 9 December enemy activity had greatly increased before the 206th Infantry Division. The artillery bombardment directed against these divisions, the long-range artillery fire on the city centre of Vitebsk, and the reappearance of rocket batteries all indicated that the offensive would start at any moment. It was therefore strange that the Soviets did not begin this attack simultaneously with the one on 13 December from the Nevel breakthrough area. Whether the enemy had not yet completed his preparations to the east of Vitebsk by this date, or whether he wanted to entice the panzer army to withdraw forces from the eastern sector to the northern one, remained unclear. Our surveillance in the next few days confirmed that the attack east of Vitebsk would soon commence, so we made an effort to disrupt the assembly of enemy infantry and tanks, as well as of his new battery positions. On 18 December, enemy adjustment fire was placed on the 206th and 14th Infantry Divisions, and this became a one-and-a-half-hour heavy barrage early on 19 December. Towards 8 am, enemy infantry, initially accompanied by 60 tanks, launched their attack against the 14th Infantry Division. They struck a 12-kilometre stretch of the right wing of the division. By the end of the day, the enemy had penetrated the front in two locations and had steadily poured trucks with infantry reinforcements into them, though our artillery emplacements managed to bring them to a halt. This was a great defensive success in view of the immense superiority of the enemy. One Hornet and two Tiger companies were sent overnight by the high command of the panzer army to reinforce the 14th Infantry Division. There were no additional reserves.

The 14th Infantry Division, under the command of Major-General Hermann Flörke, achieved another great defensive success the next day. Although our localised attacks did not penetrate the large offensive front of the enemy, we were able to foil his plan of breaking through to the Vitebsk–Surazh road. Our Tigers and Hornets played a key role on this day in destroying 60 enemy tanks and in rendering immobile another four. Lieutenant Albert Ernst of the 1st Company of the 519th Heavy Panzerjäger Battalion (Hornets) alone destroyed 14 enemy tanks. The enemy suffered high losses in men and materiel. However, our losses were also considerable. The situation remained volatile as a result, first, of our decreasing combat strength and, second, of the fact that the enemy would continue his offensive despite the losses he had suffered on this day. We anticipated that he would attack from the southeast of Vitebsk, but our reserves were severely limited.

In the early hours of 21 December, the Soviets resumed their offensive along the entire sector, albeit with less infantry and fewer tanks owing to our efforts on the previous two days. In contrast, enemy artillery fire had become somewhat stronger. The existing line was just about held through fierce fighting, thereby preventing a major breakthrough. Only in the evening was it possible for the enemy to push back the left cornerstone of the breakthrough position, which was north of Lake Vymno, to the Vitebsk–Surazh road.

Against expectations, the enemy ceased his offensive against the 14th Infantry Division on 22 December, obviously because his casualties had been severe in the last three days. His territorial gain of three to five kilometres across a width of approximately 12 kilometres was insignificant. However, enemy reinforcements were arriving, and there was no doubt that the offensive against the 14th Infantry Division would resume and that stronger attacks would commence against the adjoining wings of the 246th and 206th Infantry Divisions.

This is exactly what transpired the next morning. A particularly difficult day was in store. After half an hour of heavy preparatory fire, the Soviets, with armoured support, charged forward on either side of the boundary between the 246th and 206th Infantry Divisions. At the same time, they resumed their offensive against the right sector of the 14th Infantry Division after a one-hour heavy barrage. With two divisions and more than 20 tanks, the enemy thrust from the south to the Vitebsk–Surazh road.

Thus, the third phase of the Battle of Vitebsk had begun. The enemy reached our artillery emplacements, but by defending fiercely and counterthrusting repeatedly, we were able to constrict, or even seal off in a makeshift manner, several points of penetration. Only south of the Vitebsk–Liozno road did enemy tanks push through our artillery line towards the west. On this day, our armour-piercing weapons achieved excellent results. In the vicinity of the VI Corps, 71 enemy tanks were destroyed and four were captured. This was an indication of the severity of the battle. Given the ongoing reinforcements that the enemy was receiving in the breakthrough area, and given our own weakness, the situation remained extremely tense on the following day. The only reinforcements that could be provided for the VI Corps by the panzer army were three infantry battalions and the engineer battalion of the 197th Infantry Division.

The further conduct of battle on the northern front, and the forthcoming enemy attack on the northwestern front (Maps 7 and 9)

To the north and to the northwest of Vitebsk, the situation had very much come to a head. On the evening of 19 December, a number of trucks were coming from the northwest along the roads leading to Gorodok. The enemy closely pursued our withdrawal on the night of 19/20 December to the Shishkovo–Lake Chernovo line. On 20 December, we repelled all of the attacks against the 3rd Luftwaffe Field Division and the 20th Panzer Division. That night, the northern front of the LIII Corps fell back to the so-called northern defensive line connecting Chistopolye, Kozyrevo, and Lake Kosho. Despite the pressure applied by the enemy, the withdrawal proceeded smoothly. Meanwhile, the 20th Panzer Division was transferred to panzer army reserve and sent to the region to the northwest of Ula to be refitted and refreshed. In the area of the 3rd Luftwaffe Field Division, the enemy, who had been attacking since noon, managed to penetrate the front in two locations. The situation remained unclear in both locations for several hours, for the forces that we had committed there retreated inexplicably. Only on the next day, 22 December, was it possible to block the points of penetration and to regain the ground that had been yielded the previous day.

On 21 December, the 129th Infantry Division and the 6th Luftwaffe Field Division took over from the 252nd Infantry Division the command of the forces that were to the west and southwest of Gorodok. The troops in the Sirotino sector were to be subordinated to the headquarters of the 252nd Infantry Division. The headquarters of the IX Corps took command of all obstacle-construction units and combat forces in the sector between Sirotino and the left boundary of the panzer army. This sector was, due to the lack of forces in the previous few weeks, inadequately protected. From the beginning of December, there had been growing signs that the enemy would launch an attack here; presumably, the Soviets had initially refrained from so doing because of the difficulties of supply caused by the mud season and because of their surprising success against the northern wing of the Third Panzer Army. On 19 and 20 December, we came into contact with enemy troops in the area to the north of Sirotino. Then, for the first time, the enemy repeatedly attacked in battalion strength our combat outposts north of Sirotino on 23 December and pushed them back to the main frontline.

On this day, to the east of Vitebsk, the VI Corps had to endure combat that was tougher than ever. Meanwhile, the Soviets bombarded the northern front of the LIII Corps in the morning before launching an attack. The 3rd Luftwaffe Field Division parried a number of assaults. To the west of Kozyrevo, the enemy penetrated an area two kilometres wide and three kilometres deep. He even put under pressure the front held by a construction engineer battalion northwest and west of Gorodok, but he was kept at bay. In the evening, the enemy again pushed back a two-kilometre sector of the front southwest of Kozyrevo.

The 129th Infantry Division, severely weakened by the fierce combat that had been ongoing since 13 December, continued to suffer heavy losses. Thus, the situation on the northern front in the evening was just as tense as that on the front of the VI Corps.

'Strategy is a system of stopgaps.' This maxim by Moltke characterised our conduct at this time. Troops were moved by columns of trucks every night. Battalions that on the previous day had been fighting to the north or northeast of Vitebsk had now already moved to the east of the city. Others that had repelled the enemy in a sector of the southeast front had relocated to a different position that night, where they could count on more attacks in the morning. Nowhere could we do enough. Only a series of stopgaps were possible.

Our last reserves were in use by the LIII Corps. Enemy assaults in the area of this corps were bound to continue in the morning. Therefore, in the evening Reinhardt requested permission to withdraw those forces northwest and north of Vitebsk to the so-called Losvida defensive line between Poddubye and the northeastern tip of Lake Losvida. This sector of the front would thereby be reduced from a length of 90 kilometres to a length of 50 kilometres, and urgently needed reserves could thus be made available.

Fierce combat along the front of the panzer army on Christmas Eve (Maps 6, 9, and 10)

A decision by the Führer on our request for a withdrawal to the Losvida defensive line was still pending as dawn broke on Christmas Eve. The fighting had resumed with an alarming ferocity on all fronts, so the troops had given up any hope for a brief lull during Christmas. The situation which developed throughout the day, especially in the evening, was far more critical than anything we had undergone up to this point. Was it a coincidence that the Soviets escalated the situation along the entire front of the panzer army right on Christmas Eve, or had this been their intention?

The enemy armies that formed a circle around Vitebsk had in the meantime amassed their forces and had on this day launched a concentric attack, supported by tanks, towards the city from the southeast, east, north, and northwest. It was clear that their objective was to disrupt the lines of communication to the city and, after that, to isolate it entirely from our defensive front. The battle was now raging along the entire front of the Third Panzer Army. On several occasions, our exceptional troops were split into individual combat groups. In some locations, we had only standby units, which had constructed security lines, and supply trains. Throughout the day, the situation remained unclear in several sectors of the front. Individual battalions had been cut off from one another. Attacks and counterattacks came one after the other. The fighting was changeful, tough, and costly. Our last reserves often intercepted only those enemy forces that had thrust deep into our main defensive area. Enemy tanks were everywhere, and artillery bombardments were incessant.

Having penetrated the front on both sides of the boundary between the 246th and 206th Infantry Divisions, and having broken through our line of artillery emplacements southeast of Vitebsk, the enemy now managed to push far to the west and to the southwest. The enemy forces that we detected in this area amounted to five rifle divisions and two tank brigades. Despite temporarily successful counterattacks by individual combat groups, it was not possible until the evening to set up a solid, cohesive interdiction front along the railway line on either side of Krynki. Northwest of Krynki, enemy tanks approached the Vitebsk–Liozno railway line and threatened the Vitebsk–Orsha road to its west. All that stood in the way of these tanks were supply trains and standby units. There was a growing danger that the front would collapse here. Reinhardt therefore requested that the army group release the Panzer-Grenadier Division Feldherrnhalle. The army group refused to do so on the grounds that this division was still being trained and that it was, as a result, not yet fully operational.

The enemy continued his assault against the right sector of the 14th Infantry Division. He also took advantage of the elongated central sector by advancing on the northern side of the Vitebsk–Surazh road. Enemy forces crossed over this road on the right sector, and we attempted to push them back by maintaining the momentum of the counterattack that we had begun on 23 December. However, this failed due to the immense strength of the enemy onslaught. Nonetheless, the frontline in this sector was held. In the central sector of the division, which lay to the north of the road, the Soviets, supported by tanks, managed a three-kilometre-wide advance of up to three kilometres in depth. We brought this advance to a halt with our last reserves. By now, the division was facing 12 rifle divisions, one rifle brigade, and six armoured units.

The situation was developing most ominously in the Gorodok combat zone. With the vastly superior forces of the 11th Guards Army and of the 5th Tank Corps, the enemy pierced, in multiple locations, the painstakingly developed defensive front between Peredelki and the north of Gorodok. The 129th Infantry Division was worn out by many days of nonstop defensive fighting, and the 3rd Luftwaffe Field Division was also significantly weakened. Consequently, it had become impossible for these divisions to stop the Soviet advance towards the south. A systematic defence had been made considerably more difficult by enemy tanks punching through our columns overnight and thrusting towards the eastern and northern sides of Gorodok. In the morning, after fierce street fighting, the town fell into enemy hands. An attempt by the Soviets to push further was initially prevented by a swiftly established defensive line south of Gorodok.

By noon, after much back-and-forth communication between Reinhardt and Busch, the latter had authorised a second-line security garrison consisting, in addition to a battery, of the reconnaissance battalion of the Panzer-Grenadier Division Feldherrnhalle. These troops would be positioned southwest of Lake Losvida, not far from their quarters.

The situation further deteriorated for the panzer army owing to an offensive by the 4th Soviet Shock Army in the Gorodok–Sirotino area. Such an offensive had been brewing for several days, and it struck the boundary between the LIII and IX Corps. The enemy advanced on a wide front between Zakhody and Cheremkha. He attacked the narrow sector of the 6th Luftwaffe Field Division and the right wing of the IX Corps, penetrated deep into our main defensive area with infantry and tanks, and charged with tanks on either side of Filipenki over the Vitebsk–Sirotino road. Our weakened forces secured a line of strongpoints between Zakhody and the northwestern end of Lake Zaronovskoye as well as another in the lake-dotted area just to the east of Filipenki, although the enemy punched southwards through the latter late in the afternoon. In the sector of the IX Corps, two Soviet regiments with tanks threw our own security troops back to Gryada and to the west, necessitating the abandonment of Cheremkha and the territory to its west. A counterattack by elements of the 20th Panzer Division from the west towards Gryada was ineffective because the terrain made the positioning of heavy weaponry most difficult.

Towards 1:30 pm, we received the decision of the Führer on our request of the previous day. The northeast front (the 14th Infantry Division, the 4th and 3rd Luftwaffe Field Divisions, and the 129th Infantry Division) would be permitted to withdraw to the Losvida defensive line after nightfall.

Throughout the afternoon, to the southeast of Vitebsk, the front on the left wing of the 246th Infantry Division was on the verge of breaking into pieces. Reinhardt once again requested permission to use the Panzer-Grenadier Division Feldherrnhalle for a counterattack at this particularly vulnerable point. This was rejected by the army group. Apparently, the panzer army would have to cope alone. However, the army group did approve the use of the division to counterattack in the vicinity of Sirotino. We urgently needed this division, even though its soldiers, who hardly knew their weapons, had yet to see combat! The division had barely received the relevant preliminary order when the OKH informed us shortly before 5:30 pm that the 5th Jäger Division would now be at the disposal of the panzer army. The OKH would then move the 12th Infantry Division to the spot vacated by the 5th Jäger Division. Thus, the question remained as to whether the Feldherrnhalle could be sent to aid the VI Corps. Colonel-General Reinhardt suggested that the danger to the northwest of Vitebsk be accepted, for the front at that moment was more likely to be fractured to the southeast of the city. Enemy forces to the northwest could probably still be delayed by battalion groups of the 87th Infantry Division and by elements of the 5th Jäger Division until the Feldherrnhalle was free to counterattack in the vicinity of Sirotino. In response, the army group agreed to allow the Feldherrnhalle to be employed for a northward attack from Krynki.

Thus, the entire panzer army was either engaged in combat or on the move on Christmas Eve. It was a painful yet unavoidable situation in which the panzer army found itself. Snow fell incessantly. The Holy Night was forgotten amidst all the worry, telephone calls, and brooding. Much would be sung in the Fatherland about the battles of this day. We were under immense pressure, and our concerns about what the next day might bring meant that we felt little Christmas cheer. And yet, to be heard at some point and from somewhere in this long night was our old German Christmas carol, 'Silent Night'. It was particularly difficult for us to have to report on this evening that Major Erich Loewe, a recipient of the Knight's Cross, whose 501st Heavy Panzer Battalion (Tigers) had disabled innumerable tanks, was missing in action in the sector of the 14th Infantry Division. In his honour, the great bridge over the Western Dvina that was still under construction near Beshenkovichi was later named Major Loewe Bridge.

The fighting on the first and second days of Christmastide (Maps 6, 9, 10, and 11)

On Christmas Eve, the Panzer-Grenadier Division Feldherrnhalle rolled forward in the sector of the 246th Infantry Division. From the east of Krynki, it was to advance northwards the next morning to regain lost ground and to annihilate those enemy forces that had broken through. The Soviets, despite launching multiple night raids against the 246th Infantry Division, had made only slight progress by Christmas morning.

Northwest of Vitebsk, the withdrawal to the Losvida defensive line proceeded smoothly. In the sector of the 14th Infantry Division, south of the Western Dvina, the enemy immediately sent strong forces in pursuit. In contrast, to the northwest of the river and up to Lake Losvida, the Soviets pursued our troops only hesitantly, probably because they had concentrated the bulk of their forces from this sector on the seizure of Gorodok.

On 25 December, the enemy pressure against the left wing of the 246th Infantry Division continued unabated. Fighting hard, we prevented the enemy from breaking through to the other side of the Vitebsk–Orsha road. Difficulties in the assembly of the Panzer-Grenadier Division Feldherrnhalle caused delays until 12:30 pm. The division then attacked from the area southeast of Krynki, inflicting heavy losses on the enemy and throwing him back one and a half kilometres to the north. Unfortunately, the situation remained tense here.

Northwest of Vitebsk, the enemy, despite his quantitative superiority, made only small territorial gains in the breakthrough area east of Sirotino. It would be the task of the 5th Jäger Division in the coming days to launch an attack from the area southeast of Sirotino against the deep flank of the enemy forces advancing along the Sirotino–Vitebsk road in order to regain the ground that had been lost between Zakhody and Cheremkha.

The attack of the Feldherrnhalle continued into the early hours of the second day of Christmastide, but it made little further progress due to fierce enemy resistance and to the great difficulties presented by the terrain. The purpose of this attack had been to create new reserves and to deal with the development of the situation on the boundary between the 246th and 206th Infantry Divisions. The Feldherrnhalle was placed behind this boundary so as to repulse – or at least intercept – the enemy forces advancing westwards. On both sides of the boundary, fierce fighting continued until evening without interruption between the Vitebsk–Liozno railway line and the Vitebsk–Orsha road, as well as northeast of the railway. In the afternoon, 20 enemy tanks penetrated almost as far as the main road leading west. Just to the south of the Western Dvina, in the sector of the 14th Infantry Division, where elements of the 197th Infantry Division were being employed, the enemy managed a two-kilometre-deep breakthrough. A combat team that had initially been encircled here fought its way out to German lines in the evening. During the afternoon, the 197th Infantry Division was in action in the sector of the 14th Infantry Division. The protruding inner wings of the VI and LIII Corps on either side of the Western Dvina were withdrawn.

All enemy attacks against the northern front were deflected. The 6th Luftwaffe Field Division, under the leadership of Lieutenant-General Rudolf Peschel, survived a day filled with heavy defensive fighting. In the evening, the entire front of the division was held by only a few strongpoints, and the right wing was pushed back three kilometres. Particularly critical was the development of the situation in the area southeast of Sirotino, where the 5th Jäger Division made negligible progress against increasingly stiff enemy resistance. South of Filipenki, the enemy, with cavalry and tanks of divisional strength, pushed further southwards through dense woodlands towards the Vitebsk–Polotsk railway, striking it with artillery and explosives. The IX Corps was ordered to advance along the southern side of the chain of lakes in the direction of the southwestern tip of Lake Zaronovskoye with the aim of closing the gap to the 6th Luftwaffe Field Division. This advance was scheduled for 27 December. It would be spearheaded by the 5th Jäger Division, and would be safeguarded by our defences northeast and east of Sirotino.

The forces of the panzer army were now at a significant numerical disadvantage. Their combat strength was decreasing dramatically. Even though the army group had sent reserves (i.e. the 131st Infantry Division), they arrived only very gradually at a rate of three trains per day. Meanwhile, our intelligence indicated that the enemy still had the 10th Guards Army in reserve to the northeast of Surazh. The headquarters of the panzer army therefore submitted a detailed situation report to the army group on the evening of 26 December. It outlined the intentions of the enemy. From the southeast of Vitebsk, he would thrust westwards over the Luchesa to disrupt the Vitebsk–Orsha railway. From the northwest of the city, he would advance over the Polotsk–Vitebsk railway, which had already been temporarily interrupted on this day, in a southerly direction over the Western Dvina in order to bar the only east–west road link, Lepel–Vitebsk. If Vitebsk were to be held, and if the supply of the panzer army were to continue, it was essential that we maintain possession of a railway line and of at least one east–west road link. Because of our alarmingly low combat strength, in particular that of the LIII Corps, and because of the deteriorating physical and mental state of our troops, the high command of the panzer army believed that, with the forces currently available, the situation northwest of Vitebsk could hardly be overcome. We therefore requested, at the very least, that the 12th Infantry Division, which was going to be sent to the area northeast of Polotsk, be used instead on the right wing of the IX Corps and that another division be allocated to the Polotsk area.

The fighting on the last days of 1943 (Maps 6, 10, and 12)

We had confirmed that the Soviets were now enveloping Vitebsk with at least 37 rifle divisions, three cavalry divisions, 15 armoured units, and four mechanised brigades. Nonetheless, we withstood the multiple assaults that they launched on 27 December. Since 19 December, the day of the beginning of the offensive (i.e. nine days), the enemy had lost 355 tanks. The counterattacks by the Feldherrnhalle and the 5th Jäger Division against those enemy forces that had broken through brought partial success. Even though the Polotsk–Vitebsk railway had become impassable since the day before, the Vitebsk–Orsha road, which had been under threat for several days, remained firmly in our hands.

It was the courage and personal bravery of every single officer and enlisted man that enabled us to fend off a numerically superior enemy again and again.

There was nonstop enemy activity at the boundary of the 246th and 206th Infantry Divisions. We observed infantry and vehicle movements throughout the day. The Soviets also constantly sent reinforcements to the breakthrough area east of Sirotino. By the evening, the position of the enemy was such that we were most concerned about how the situation might develop the next day. One ray of hope was provided by the 12th Infantry Division, which had been made available for an attack to be carried out that evening by the IX Corps southeast of Sirotino.

Overnight, southeast of Vitebsk, Soviet tanks drove right up to the Vitebsk–Orsha road. During the morning of 28 December, the Feldherrnhalle, now located where the right sector of the 206th Infantry Division had been, hurled back these enemy tanks so far to the east that, from noon onwards, the road could again be used. Meanwhile, the 246th Infantry Division repeatedly repelled the breakthrough attempts of the enemy forces that had arrived the day before. The fighting was fierce and costly for both sides. The concentration of artillery firepower by the 206th Infantry Division hindered the enemy advance. On the northern front, there was a lull in the fighting. The enemy had been brought to a standstill across a broad front between Lakes Losvida and Zaronovskoye, though not before he had advanced up to four kilometres in the woodlands west of Lake Losvida. The counterattack of the 5th Jäger Division southeast of Sirotino saw only minor territorial gain, but it succeeded in tying down strong enemy forces and preventing their dreaded lunge towards the south.

Towards noon, the army group authorised the overnight withdrawal of our troops still north and west of Lake Losvida. The eastern and southern banks of this lake would now form the frontline. Reserves could thereby be made available for the weak, albeit outstanding, 6th Luftwaffe Field Division on both sides of Lake Zaronovskoye. During the night, the 5th Jäger Division regrouped in the vicinity of Zavyazye. In conjunction with a regimental group of the 12th Infantry Division and two heavy rocket projector battalions, it was to attack on 29 December towards the northeast in order to close the gap near Yermachki.

The defensive combat in these days intensified in several locations, with our troops displaying the utmost heroism. Amidst light frost and snowfall, the winter battle for Vitebsk seemed to have reached its critical stage. It was only now that everything was truly being done to assist the panzer army. Those 'above' had finally realised that the Vitebsk region had become *the* focal point of the Eastern Front. On this day, Field-Marshal Busch appealed to the three other armies of the army group to help voluntarily and to hand over to us what they could. Our right-hand neighbour, the Fourth Army, initially sent a reinforced obstacle-construction unit to the sector of the VI Corps, for which we were especially grateful. Such help from an army which was similarly embroiled in fierce fighting showed that our armies were closely united in this difficult struggle.

On the three final days of the year, the enemy remobilised his troops at multiple points in an effort to reach his objective. Yet his push against us was futile. All his attacks were repelled, and he occasionally had to relinquish the territory he had gained.

In the breakthrough area southeast of Vitebsk, the enemy pressure against the right wing of the 206th Infantry Division increased considerably. Despite his heavy preparatory fire (10,000 to 12,000 rounds of all calibres), the enemy was kept at bay. Any forces that broke through were annihilated. The Soviets renewed their assault the following day, in part with fresh forces. They managed a westward advance just beyond the Vitebsk–Orsha road, but shortly thereafter we disabled 15 of their tanks, compelling them to reverse their course. The casualties suffered by the enemy over the previous few days had been so great that, by the last day of 1943, his attack in this sector lost any sense of coordination. The counterattack of the Feldherrnhalle and of the obstacle-construction unit of the Fourth Army pushed the front one kilometre to the east of the Vitebsk–Orsha road.

The fighting subsided in the sector south of the Western Dvina (the 14th and 197th Infantry Divisions) and on the northern front up to Lake Losvida. Southwest of Lake Losvida, the enemy repeatedly struck the new front of the LIII Corps, but he did so in vain. He again focused his attack against the right sector of the 6th Luftwaffe Field Division, but any penetration was swiftly dealt with.

On 29 December, the 5th Jäger Division and the bulk of the 12th Infantry Division began their northeastward advance from the Zavyazye area. After three days of fierce combat, they reached the high ground near the southwestern tip of Lake Zaronovskoye, almost cutting off the enemy forces that had broken through to the railway line. We planned to continue the advance the next day until the gap was finally closed.

In the breakthrough area southeast of Vitebsk, the front had come as close as nine kilometres to the headquarters of the panzer army. The headquarters was therefore relocated to Beshenkovichi, on the

Lepel–Vitebsk road, on 30 and 31 December. It was set up in a large two-storey stone house, which had served as Napoleon's accommodation for two nights during his march on Moscow in 1812.

It snowed heavily on the last two nights of the year. Only now was the Russian winter really setting in. There was a brief pause in the fighting at the start of the New Year. After the success of the last couple of days, the great danger to the northwest of Vitebsk seemed to have been averted. Southeast of the city, it still appeared to be dangerous. Nonetheless, our success in defending the entire front of the panzer army in the preceding few weeks inspired confidence in our ability to obtain a favourable outcome in the end. We still had to stand firm for a few days until sufficient forces arrived (including the 12th Panzer Division and the 131st and 299th Infantry Divisions) to prevent Vitebsk from being sliced off from the front of the Third Panzer Army.

1944

The fateful year of 1944 had begun. The German Eastern Army still held a vast amount of Russian territory. And yet, within six to seven months, the collapse of Army Group Centre was to commence with the destruction of the Third Panzer Army. After almost another four weeks, the rest of the army group would lose 380,000 men, but would just manage keep the Soviets off German soil. Yet such a scenario was unimaginable at the start of the year. The fighting spirit of the troops was unbroken. Our successful defence had re-awoken a feeling of superiority despite the overwhelming numerical strength of the enemy. Even though there had been major setbacks in the previous year, we remained convinced that the struggle against the Soviet Union could be decided in our favour.

After the collapse of Army Group Centre, it was often falsely claimed that the war in the east had already been hopelessly lost due to the difficulties in holding the front, and that it was only the leadership, only the generals, who had eagerly sought to continue the fighting. Such claims are nonsensical given that the German soldier in the east still fought with the utmost heroism in 1944. He believed that we would triumph in this struggle, and was determined to protect the Fatherland from the Bolsheviks.

The combat around Vitebsk in the first few days of 1944 (Maps 6 and 10)

During the winter defensive battle for Vitebsk that had now been ongoing for 19 days, the Soviets had assembled at least 52 rifle divisions, five rifle brigades, three cavalry divisions, and 22 armoured units against the front of the Third Panzer Army. By way of compensation for his significant casualties, the enemy had not only sent a steady stream of replacements to the front but had also thrown a large number of penal companies into combat. Nevertheless, operational successes eluded him.

Heavy snowstorms and temperatures as low as six degrees below zero meant that there was less combat activity on the first four days of the New Year than there had been during the previous few days. Some enemy forces had successfully renewed their advance towards the Vitebsk–Orsha road in the area of the VI Corps, but they were destroyed in a counterattack. So as to provide further support to this threatened sector of the front, the newly-arrived 131st Infantry Division was inserted between the Feldherrnhalle and the 206th Infantry Division. The 246th Infantry Division repelled multiple assaults, even though the enemy had preceded them with one hour of preparatory fire. Northwest of Vitebsk, the 129th Infantry Division resisted several strikes southwest of Lake Losvida, sometimes in close combat. The 6th Luftwaffe Field Division, despite its best efforts, was unable to prevent a Soviet advance to the northwest tip of Lake Zaronovskoye. Given that there were insufficient forces for a counterthrust, the left wing of the division had to be withdrawn one kilometre. In the area of the IX Corps, the 5th Jäger Division forged ahead, albeit slowly, against strong enemy resistance. The right wing of the division took Yermachki and almost reached the southwestern tip of Lake Zaronovskoye. Yet an armoured counterattack by the Soviets threw the division back to the heights one kilometre to the southwest, thereby enabling the continued supply to those enemy forces in the breakthrough area.

Because the fighting had abated in the first few days of January, we were under the impression that the defensive battle was nearing its end. Then, quite unexpectedly on 5 January, the great battle was renewed on all fronts. This day proved to be the most difficult to date in the battle of Vitebsk. Southeast of the city, the enemy, having laid down intense preparatory fire, resumed his offensive in the entire breakthrough area. Concealed by the mist, the enemy advanced up to two kilometres to the west of the highway, deep into the left flank of the Feldherrnhalle. The ground that had been lost was shortly regained in a determined counterattack by the 1st Battalion of the 481st Grenadier Regiment, 256th Infantry Division. This battalion had already played a decisive role in the few days beforehand, preventing an enemy penetration of the front. Northwest of Vitebsk, the 6th Luftwaffe Field Division found itself at the centre of an enemy offensive overnight and during the day. South of Lake Zaronovskoye, the Soviets sought to advance further towards the southeast. Owing to the heroic fighting of our troops and the use of our last reserves, all enemy attacks were warded off.

On 6 January, the enemy significantly reinforced his position to make a massive push in the direction of Vitebsk from the southeast and from the northwest. With closely coordinated forces, as well as the strongest artillery and air support, he focused his attack against the right wing of the 206th Infantry Division and the northwestern front of the LIII Corps. Indeed, between Lakes Losvida and Zaronovskoye, both the 129th Infantry Division and the 6th Luftwaffe Field Division had to put up the most tenacious defence possible. After one-and-a-half hours of preparatory fire, the enemy launched a follow-up attack of up to regimental strength. Yet, despite his employment of ground-attack aircraft, his numerous attempts to penetrate the front failed. He lost 49 tanks in the process.

South of Lake Zaronovskoye, the enemy carried out multiple assaults, albeit in vain. The 5th Jäger Division renewed its push towards Yermachki, but enemy resistance was overwhelming. The situation there had become much more difficult, for the Soviets had sent new forces into the breakthrough area on the boundary between the LIII and IX Corps. Reinhardt therefore abandoned any further efforts to strangulate these forces and reorganised the IX Corps so as to fortify and straighten out the front. Field-Marshal Busch initially objected to this decision, but he eventually had to approve it on the grounds that nothing could be done about the newly arrived enemy forces. During the night of 6/7 January, the troops that had been striving to reach Yermachki were withdrawn. This enabled the detachment of those elements of the 12th Infantry Division that had been in use here. With the entire 12th Infantry Division, we intended to carve out a new front along the Slobodka–Chystsi line on 8 January.

A new enemy army, probably the 5th, moved into position for a revival of the offensive southeast of Vitebsk. Limiting himself to smaller raids in this vicinity on 7 January, he made only a small dent in the front of the 206th Infantry Division.

The enemy applied further pressure against the left wing of the LIII Corps all night and all day. The troops of the 129th Infantry Division and the 6th Luftwaffe Field Division, despite being severely weakened by the nonstop fighting of the last few days and nights, continued to exert themselves to the utmost. Early in the morning, the infantry of the 6th Luftwaffe Field Division still amounted to 436 men. There were heavy losses on both sides, but we held our position in most locations. However, our casualties were so great southwest of Lake Losvida that the Soviets managed to pierce the front near Matrassy. Towards noon, they stood on the northern bank of Lake Zaronovskoye. The encircled western wing of the 6th Luftwaffe Field Division held out all day long and, as ordered, fought its way back to our lines in the evening. The LIII Corps then received the order to establish a new frontline on 8 January with the 6th Luftwaffe Field Division and the 12th Infantry Division between Bondarevo and the southern tip of the great forest to the north of Uzhlyatsina.

Assessment of the situation prior to further combat (Maps 6 and 10)

In the middle of the day of 7 January, Field-Marshal Busch met with Colonel-General Reinhardt at the command post of the IX Corps. Reinhardt took the opportunity to report the following:

The Soviets are pushing towards Vitebsk with three armies from the east and another three from the northwest. On operational grounds, and for reasons of prestige, their objective is undoubtedly the seizure of the city. There is no sign as to what the subsequent operational intentions of the enemy might be. He is still throwing all of his reserves against Vitebsk. He has a new army approaching from the east, and another seems to be coming from the north. He is certainly suffering heavy casualties, but he remains capable of replacing them quickly with brand new units.

It is clearly the task of the panzer army to hold Vitebsk, the cornerstone of the entire front. This task is made difficult not so much by the numerical superiority of the enemy as by the ever-decreasing fighting power of our own forces. The men on the Soviet side, who are always able to be replaced or relieved by fresh troops, stand opposite the German troops, who for months on end, day in and day out, have fought nonstop. Our men have even had to fend off night raids recently. They are simply overexerted. Their numbers are falling drastically, and it is thanks to their willpower alone that they can still hold out.

Until now, we have received sufficient replacements for our losses, but this can no longer be expected to continue in future. The panzer army will foreseeably have to fulfil its current tasks with the forces currently at its disposal. It will be necessary to keep the front intact and to prevent further casualties. Our losses have already been high as a result of some units in protruding positions becoming isolated from the rest of the front, as is the case now in the area of the LIII Corps.

It would therefore be best to shorten certain sectors of the front in due course, especially if our forces continue to weaken. We do not want to put too much at stake and sacrifice that which cannot easily be replaced. This will require some troops to give up their reinforced positions and move out into the open country. Only a few divisions remain in these positions. New trenches, defensive lines, and fortifications are under construction further to the rear. It need hardly be feared that our troops would let too much ground 'slip from their grasp', as is repeatedly claimed by those 'above'. Everyone is aware of the importance of holding Vitebsk.

I therefore consider it necessary that the panzer army be prepared to hold onto Vitebsk under all circumstances. So that this can be done, the panzer army must be given the freedom to shorten any sector of the front that becomes overstretched.

Field-Marshal Busch replied:

Holding out is our primary duty; falling back is forbidden. The divisional commanders and the troops under their command might be tempted to withdraw whenever they suffer casualties. Only the corps commanders may request that the frontline be shortened, but approval must be given by the panzer army or by the army group. Any major changes must be decided by the OKH.

Even so, Busch generally seemed to be in agreement with Reinhardt's assessment.

Reinhardt then proposed that the intended advance to the northwest part of Lake Zaronovskoye by the 12th Infantry Division be abandoned and that the 299th Infantry Division be concentrated not immediately southeast of Vitebsk but behind the sector of the Feldherrnhalle. This division could be made ready for a rapid counterattack against the enemy should he display a moment's weakness, thereby preventing him from reaching the so very vital Vitebsk–Orsha railway. Busch agreed with both proposals.

The tough defensive battles of 8 and 9 January 1944 (Maps 6 and 10)

Early on 8 January, after an hour-long heavy barrage, the enemy counter-attacked with his new infantry and armoured units. These units probably belonged to the 5th Army, and with close air support they struck the Feldherrnhalle and the left wing of the 246th Infantry Division. We fought hard and lost 57 tanks, but prevented a breakthrough by the much stronger enemy, who had temporarily pushed as far as the Luchesa. Nonetheless, the north–south road in the sector of the Feldherrnhalle was now in enemy hands. A two-kilometre gap had opened up between this division and the 131st Infantry Division. A counterattack by the latter sought to close this gap, but the division soon ground to a halt under enemy barrage fire. Out in the open, our infantry, artillery, and rocket-projector units distinguished themselves in defending their positions. In cooperation with our air units, they crushed the enemy's attempts to make preparations, to concentrate his troops, and to send in new formations. Northwest of Krynki alone, we observed and fought against several thousand men and more than 100 tanks. The 299th Infantry Division was assembled on the Luchesa in readiness to launch an attack, although it would only be carried out if the enemy pushed further west on 9 January.

The fighting northwest of Vitebsk had been ongoing for several days, and at this time it still continued relentlessly. The enemy made the situation particularly difficult by delivering more than 1000 airstrikes. 30 of his tanks were put out of action in the course of the day (out of a total of 87 in the entire area of the panzer army, which itself possessed only about 75 combat-ready tanks). The two battalions of the 6th Luftwaffe Field Division that had been encircled the previous day managed to extricate themselves overnight. A gap had opened up between the 3rd Luftwaffe Field Division and the combat command of the 129th Infantry Division, on this day subordinated to the 6th Luftwaffe Field Division. This gap was still open the evening. The 12th Infantry Division came under the command of the LIII Corps due to the shift of the corps boundary to the Uzhlyatsina area.

There was a heavy snowstorm southeast of Vitebsk on 9 January, and the Soviets attempted fruitlessly to lunge further westwards from the advanced position that they had established the previous night in the right sector of the Feldherrnhalle. Our troops, though weak and overextended, held this sector against all attacks, destroying 60 enemy tanks and immobilising another 27. The Hornets of the 519th Heavy Panzerjäger Battalion played a preeminent role in this regard. In view of the snowstorm and the large snowdrifts, we withheld the order for an attack by the 299th Infantry Division.

We all felt that our fate would be decided at Vitebsk. Yet we were also confident in our ability to hold out. The exertions and deprivations of the combat troops were incredible. All of our forces were strained day and night to the utmost. The mutual trust between the combat troops and the leadership of the panzer army continually provided fresh impetus. Moreover, the troops had complete faith in the commander of the panzer army, Colonel-General Reinhardt. A strong bond had been forged in the fighting of the last few weeks. Vitebsk had come to mean a great deal to all of us. Fifty-six rifle divisions, five rifle brigades, three cavalry divisions, and 22 armoured units now confronted our 14 infantry divisions, one jäger division, one panzer-grenadier division, and two panzer divisions.

Measures taken to construct rearward positions (Map 12)

On 9 January, the headquarters of the Third Panzer Army issued two important orders, whose timely and correct execution decisively influenced the course of events over the summer.

The first order dealt with the accelerated construction of emplacements and defensive positions with all available construction units. Most important was the Tiger Line, which was to be the new frontline should Vitebsk be lost. It ran from Lake Orekhi to the bend in the Western Dvina northeast of Beshenkovichi and further to another bend in the river southwest of Polotsk. Considerable forces could be saved southeast of Vitebsk, where the line followed a distinct chain of lakes. We ordered that top priority be given to its construction south of the Western Dvina. Aside from the Tiger Line, we ordered the construction of a number of defensive positions, which would help hold Vitebsk. We intended these defensive positions to be ready by spring, and the Tiger Line by the end of May.

The second order concerned itself with the defence of Vitebsk. It stated that the city was to be provided with all the means necessary to withstand an enemy assault: 'If, in the course of the winter battle around Vitebsk, the city should fall within the immediate combat zone, the responsibility for its defence will be passed to the headquarters of the VI Corps. The corps shall then assign a divisional commander to the city.'

As we will see later, the most senior commanders subsequently altered this order so significantly that the catastrophe was bound to befall the Third Panzer Army only a few days after the commencement of the Soviet summer offensive.

The last few days of the first defensive battle (Maps 6 and 10)

On 10 January in the combat zone of southeast Vitebsk, the enemy ground to a halt. He had pushed beyond the Vitebsk–Orsha road, but had been checked elsewhere in this sector. There was a revival of combat activity in only a few places along the rest of the front of the panzer army on this day.

The enemy had expanded the salient southwest of Vitebsk overnight, but he soon had to go over to the defensive. The 299th Infantry Division, reinforced with tanks and self-propelled assault guns, and weak elements of the 131st Infantry Division launched an attack from the southwest and the northwest. In the face of stubborn enemy resistance, we managed to retake only two towns, both of which had already changed hands twice that day. Enemy artillery fire, armoured defence, and counterattacks hindered further progress. His losses were high, with 61 tanks and 15 antitank guns destroyed during the day. Yet our losses were also severe.

Of the few remaining engagements along the rest of the front of the panzer army, that in which the 6th Luftwaffe Field Division participated was especially difficult, for the division failed to establish a continuous defensive front in the wooded terrain.

The number of enemy tanks that the panzer army had put out of action since 13 December 1943 had now risen to 1,023, of which 949 had been destroyed. A single onslaught by 28 partially-refitted enemy armoured units had been smashed to smithereens. Lance Corporal Albert, from one of our panzerjäger battalions, was at this time awarded the Knight's Cross of the Iron Cross for disabling 24 tanks.

On 12 January, the Soviets, after preparatory artillery fire and with armoured and air support, continued their attempt to envelop Vitebsk, especially from the northwest. At 13 degrees below zero, this day proved to be a complete defensive success, especially for our infantry, who had been fighting fiercely for weeks on end. They were supported effectively by our artillery, rocket projectors, armour-piercing weapons, and air force. The solidarity between the various branches of the armed forces was demonstrative of true comradeship. Every branch had done all that was possible to relieve the heavy burden that had been carried by the infantry. All enemy assaults either crumbled in the face of our defensive fire or were repulsed by our counterattacks.

On the morning of 13 January, the enemy assembled about six rifle divisions and two tank brigades opposite the 6th Luftwaffe Field Division and the 12th Infantry Division in readiness for a major offensive operation on both sides of Lake Zaronovskoye. He preceded his advance with exceptionally heavy preparatory fire delivered by approximately 200 batteries as well as mortars and automatic guns. They were supported by bombers and ground-attack aircraft. Once this preparatory phase was over, he moved forward along the entire front between Bondarevo and the Polotsk–Vitebsk railway line. The point of main effort of the enemy's armoured advance (about 70 tanks) lay to the south of Lake Zaronovskoye. Our infantry conducted a bold counterthrust, brilliantly supported not only by our artillery but also by our dive bombers – nine raids were performed by Stukas with the utmost precision. The infantry fought heroically, often with cold steel, to stave off the enemy. 20 of his tanks were destroyed, three of them in close combat. With the exception of a single point of penetration south of Lake Zaronovskoye, the front-line in the northwest sector stood fast. The Hornets of the 519th Heavy Panzerjäger Battalion had now been in action for 25 days, and by this time the number of enemy tanks that they had immobilised reached 205.

Presumably because of his substantial losses on this day, the enemy carried out only a few isolated attacks over the next couple of days. However, on 14 January, the enemy struck the 246th Infantry Division with artillery, tanks, and aircraft. He suffered heavy casualties in the central and western sectors of the division. At its eastern corner, though, the enemy pushed forward two kilometres.

From 15 January, there was no noteworthy action northwest of Vitebsk. Instead, the Soviets continued to apply pressure southeast of the city. Enemy tanks, with their point of main effort immediately to the west of Krynki, attacked the northern sector of the 246th Infantry Division. They managed to advance three kilometres before being stopped just to the north of Cherkassy. Driving forward another two-and-a-half kilo-metres, they reached the northern perimeter of the town. The enemy forces here and in the area to the southeast of the town were almost completely destroyed when we counterattacked on 17 January. On this final day of the first defensive battle around Vitebsk, the 246th Infantry Division destroyed 36 enemy tanks. Altogether, the Soviets had lost 88 tanks since the start of their advance on 14 January.

The headquarters of the panzer army was now able to report that the defensive combat that had broken out on the northern wing on 13 December 1943, which in the last few weeks had transformed into the defensive battle for Vitebsk, had been brought to a temporary conclusion.

On 18 January, there was a revival of active combat in the sector of the 246th Infantry Division. Yet the enemy's assaults were uncoordin-ated and lacking in striking power. Even if he managed to pierce the front southwest of Krynki, we would be able to neutralise him with an immediate counterthrust. Such was the case on the left wing of the division. After briefly losing Dribino to a Soviet battalion of 14 tanks, we inflicted heavy casualties on the enemy and retook the town.

Soviet combat activity abated after 19 January, even in the region south-east of Vitebsk. The first defensive battle had finally ended. Nonetheless, the new offensive intentions of the enemy northwest of the city were clearly indicated by his movement of forces from the Gorodok area to the southwest, by the heavy traffic before the front of the 12th Infantry Division, and by the noise of vehicles that we had been able to hear for several days before the left wing of this division. The thaw that had been setting in since the previous day made all movement in the combat zone more difficult. This at long last allowed the troops to rest and gave us the opportunity to reorganise our units. Due to the desperate situation, a number of battalions had found themselves fighting under the command of divisions to which they had not originally belonged.

Closing remarks on the first defensive battle for Vitebsk (Map 13)

With the following brief words, the Wehrmacht communique of 21 January made a note of the fierce fighting of the last five weeks and of the valiant effort of the troops:

> Since 13 December 1943, the troops commanded by Colonel-General Reinhardt fought hard in the major defensive battle in the area of Vitebsk. They inflicted the heaviest casualties on the enemy, thus foiling his attempt to penetrate the front with his approximately 50 rifle divisions and numerous armoured formations. Up until 18 January 1944, the Bolsheviks suffered more than 40,000 fatalities in this area. Many times that number were wounded. 1,203 enemy tanks and 349 guns have been destroyed or captured.

Only a small number can possibly understand what these words allude to: of bravery and personal courage, of camaraderie from fighter to fighter, of crises and almost hopeless situations that had been endured, and of deprivation, sacrifice, exertion, and sorrow. Yet the awareness that the Bolsheviks had been ground to a halt at the gates of Europe filled everyone with satisfaction and gratitude. For those who had partaken in the fighting, there was also a feeling of pride.

Quoted here are the most important passages from the order of the day of Army Group Centre on 22 January. This order had been issued when the first defensive battle for Vitebsk had ended, and it gave a broad, coherent account of the individual phases of this battle:

> Although the enemy, in the course of the fighting, commanded four armies (33 rifle divisions and 17 armoured units) east of Vitebsk as well as two armies (23 rifle divisions and 11 armoured units) north and northwest of the city, he achieved neither an operationally decisive breakthrough nor the seizure of Vitebsk.
>
> The battle began on 13 December 1943 with a concentric attack against the northward-protruding salient of the panzer army. After the initial breakthrough attempt from the north had been prevented by our determined resistance, the Soviet offensive expanded itself on 19 December on the front east of Vitebsk and then on 24 December on the front northwest of the city. The enemy suffered severe and bloody losses in nonstop and ever more ferocious fighting as he repeatedly sought to penetrate the eastern wing of the panzer army. He lost 759 tanks on this wing, despite the fact that our troops were completely exhausted.
>
> Northwest of Vitebsk, the enemy was prevented from breaking through the sector between Lakes Losvida and Zaronovskoye. He suffered so many casualties that he had to cease attacking on 16 January 1944.
>
> The artillery, panzer, panzerjäger, and assault artillery units, as well as the air force, played a particularly decisive role alongside the brave and tenacious grenadiers and panzer-grenadiers in our success. The enemy suffered losses which in our assessment amounted to approximately 190,000 men. In addition, 2,250 prisoners and deserters were captured and 349 guns were captured or destroyed. The disabling of 1,203 tanks, of which 1,114 were destroyed, indicates how severe the fighting was.

The following outline compares the forces available to both sides during the first winter defensive battle:

Our forces
- 14 infantry divisions
- 1 jäger division
- 2 panzer divisions
- 1 panzer-grenadier division
- 19 army artillery battalions
- 7 rocket projector battalions
- 7 assault artillery brigades
- 2 Tiger battalions
- 4 panzerjäger battalions (of which 2 were Hornet battalions)

Enemy forces
- 56 rifle divisions
- 5 rifle brigades
- 3 cavalry divisions
- 1 artillery division with elements of 3 more artillery divisions
- 4 army artillery regiments
- 9 guards mortar regiments
- 25 tank brigades
- 3 tank regiments

CHAPTER 13

Regrouping at the front

The subsequent two-week break from fighting would be used to reorganise our considerably mixed-up units. Most of them were re-sorted into their divisions by 29 January.

Shortly after the end of the first defensive battle, the Third Panzer Army was instructed to release some of its formations. On the order of the OKH, the 12th Panzer Division, elements of which had been deployed southwest of Lake Losvida on 18 January for the relief of the struggling 129th Infantry Division, had to be detached and assembled at Ula. This took place on 22 January. The Panzer-Grenadier Division Feldherrnhalle had already left the area of the panzer army on 17 January; the 129th Infantry Division followed suit on 22 January.

Between 24 and 28 January, the 14th and 246th Infantry Divisions exchanged their sectors of the front. From 17 January, the 211th Infantry Division rolled forward from the Polotsk region to the area of the VI Corps where, on 1 February, it took over responsibility for what had been the right sector of the 14th Infantry Division. The 3rd Luftwaffe Field Division was disbanded on 22 January and its elements were divided up between the 4th and 6th Luftwaffe Field Divisions. At the same time, the 6th Luftwaffe Field Division was assigned the sector that had previously been covered by the 3rd Luftwaffe Field Division. The 87th Infantry Division moved to where the 6th Luftwaffe Field Division had been. The 20th Panzer Division left the area of the panzer army on 28 January, but, from 31 January, parts of this division would re-enter the area of the LIII Corps, for strong enemy attacks were expected there. From 3 February, it took over the sector of the soon to be transferred 87th Infantry Division.

Thus, from this date there stood on the front eight divisions in the area of the VI Corps (256th, 211th, 14th, 299th, 131st, 206th, 246th, and 197th), four divisions in the area of the LIII Corps (4th Luftwaffe, 6th Luftwaffe, 20th Panzer, and 12th), and two divisions in the area of the IX Corps (5th Jäger and 252nd).

Also from this date, the first platoons of the 95th Infantry Division arrived in the area of the panzer army.

CHAPTER 14

The second winter defensive battle around Vitebsk, and the first signs of the fighting to come

The ground thawed in the second half of January. Combat activity died down during this time. We were increasingly concerned about enemy fire against the Vitebsk–Orsha railway line, especially given that the front had neared a major bridge along this line. Damage was being caused to the tracks with ever-greater frequency. A number of trains were derailed, losses were high, and the bridge was often in a state of disrepair for hours and even for whole days. The supply traffic and the divisions travelling along this line suffered severely.

There were indications that the enemy would soon resume his offensive, particularly northwest of Vitebsk. Enemy traffic had become heavier both southeast and northwest of the city. Moreover, he was carrying out more reconnaissance raids and artillery movements. Yet from day to day the Soviets postponed the beginning of their attack, presumably due to the blustery weather with its rain, snow, ice, and mud. The enemy did carry out a local operation south of Krynki (see Map 6), creating a two-kilometre wide penetration in the front of the 14th Infantry Division. This made necessary the withdrawal of German forces that were currently east of this position. The first major engagement took place northwest of Vitebsk on 31 January in the sector of the 5th Jäger Division. After half an hour of preparatory fire (6,000 to 8,000 rounds), the Soviets launched their attack from the east and the north, breaking through the frontline in several locations. By the evening, we had recovered these lost positions. The enemy suffered heavy losses on 2 February, as we repelled all his assaults along a 12-kilometre stretch of the front that extended on either side of Lake Zaronovskoye. The arrival of enemy infantry and tanks in this sector indicated that an offensive was imminent. Moreover, there continued to be enemy activity in the breakthrough area southeast of Vitebsk.

The first defensive battle for Vitebsk had not brought about the success the Soviets had expected, especially with their overwhelming quantitative superiority in men and materiel. In order to achieve their operational goal of advancing into the Baltic states, they would still need a secure assembly area. Specifically, they would have to seize Vitebsk to remove the threat to their flank.

After a half month break from fighting, the enemy redeployed the armies, now refreshed and resupplied, that had already taken part in the first battle. His objective was to thrust simultaneously with these six armies (the 33rd, 5th, 39th, 43rd, 11th Guards, and 4th Shock Armies) from the southeast and the northwest so as to encircle and annihilate the German troops who held the 'fortress' of Vitebsk. Soviet prisoners revealed that Vitebsk was intended to be a second Stalingrad.

The second winter defensive battle began on 3 February with the advance of the Soviet forces from their assembly points. The preparatory fire that took place beforehand was greater in strength and intensity than we had hitherto encountered. Northwest of the city, between Lakes Losvida and Zaronovskoye, the enemy lay down a heavy barrage that lasted two and a half hours. Strongly supported by air and armoured units, the first wave of his attack surged forward.

Defensive combat in the sector of the VI Corps (Map 14)

Southeast of Vitebsk, it was initially the combined forces of the 33rd Army and parts of the 39th Army (i.e. 20 rifle divisions, a rifle brigade, and six tank brigades) that moved from the Makarova–Bondari sector with lines of attack towards the west and northwest. Supported by strong artillery fire and with a constant flow of reserves, the enemy penetrated the front in multiple locations. His significant commitment of armour and reinforcements indicated that he sought to gain space as quickly as possible tothen push northwest and make contact with the 11th Guards and 4th Shock Armies. After fierce toing and froing, the entire sector that was under attack was pushed back by three kilometres. Gaps opened up at several points along the front which could only be partially covered by switch positions or security lines. But the intended enemy breakthrough was prevented and the east bank of the Luchesa remained in our hands. Soviet losses, which included at least 40 tanks, were so high that his attacks on 4 February lacked the striking power that they had possessed the previous day. These attacks mostly struck the Luchesa front. All day long, the enemy persistently tried to hurl his forces over the river. Particularly tough was the combat in the vicinity of Noviki. But all his attempts were thwarted. Only in the evening were a few weak forces able to cross the river north of Noviki.

As a result of his lack of success on the first few days, the enemy changed his approach to one which involved slicing off small pieces of the front of the VI Corps and annihilating them one by one. Those of his attacks which did not collapse immediately did eventually fail after bitter close combat against the tenacious German troops who defended the bridgeheads on the east bank of the river.

On the night of 5/6 February, the enemy launched a series of raids in the Myaklovo sector and against the Noviki bridgehead. He then brought in two divisions from neighbouring sectors so that, on 6 February, he could shift his point of main effort further north whilst maintaining pressure against the bridgeheads east of the Luchesa. Towards noon, after extremely heavy preparatory fire, he advanced on either side of the highway and railway line leading towards Vitebsk, but a counterattack of ours intercepted and contained him. Throughout the day, there was lively aerial activity along the entire front of the panzer army. Several enemy close-support aircraft struck our ground forces. Our Stukas hit a number of targets in return. Yet the enemy continued to apply ever greater pressure against us. He utilised every arm, and, as the weather improved, sent in more and more aircraft. After replacing his losses, regrouping his forces, and consolidating his armoured units, he was able to renew his assault with the utmost ruthlessness.

We were increasingly concerned about our supply. The Vitebsk–Orsha railway line had been damaged by enemy artillery on 3 February, and this had disrupted traffic for several hours. On this day, 2,900 tonnes of ammunition had been used up – the equivalent of four or five train-load. On 6 and 7 February, this section of track was repeatedly bombed, thereby completely paralysing railway traffic. The chief of supply services of the panzer army ensured that the motor transport columns drove day and night to sustain the supply to our troops, especially with regard to equipping them with ammunition. The railway engineer troops, under fire from enemy artillery, worked feverishly to repair a damaged railway bridge and to make the line passable once more. In the long run, however, the troops in both major combat zones could only be supplied by rail if traffic was running smoothly. Enemy action against the Vitebsk–Orsha line therefore had to be prevented, since supplies could no longer be delivered along the Polotsk–Vitebsk line. But the threat to our supply lines was not the only problem. The gap between both breakthrough areas was becoming ever narrower, and the only reserves we could draw on came from the curved front northeast of Vitebsk. The high command of the Third Panzer Army was therefore beginning to consider how long this protruding front to the northeast could still be held. Field-Marshal Busch, to whom Colonel-General Reinhardt made a report, rejected every suggestion that this front be withdrawn.

We repelled four enemy assaults against the Noviki bridgehead on 7 February despite the fact that he was strongly supported by armour and artillery. Any enemy forces that penetrated the front were annihilated in close combat. In this fighting, the commander of the fusilier battalion of the 131st Infantry Division, Major Ludwig Schütte, distinguished himself by demonstrating the utmost bravery. Since 3 February, he and his troops had beaten back a total of 21 enemy attacks, some of them of regimental strength, in close combat or in immediate counterattacks. Sergeant Heinrich Degener from the 431st Grenadier Regiment, who had already proven himself on 3 February as the commander of a strong point in the forest north of Myaklovo, once more demonstrated exemplary effort by eliminating enemy forces that had penetrated the front near the Noviki bridgehead. Deserving of special mention is Sergeant Josef Paulik from the 528th Grenadier Regiment who, on his own initiative and with only two men, retook crucial high ground north of Makarova, in the process doing away with 40 Soviets in close combat as well as capturing one officer and eight men.

The enemy concentrated his efforts on 3 February against the right wing of the 206th Infantry Division. He broke through this sector late in the morning, and we were only able to stop him north of Popovka.

Despite the difficulties presented by the marsh and forest terrain, we successfully thwarted Soviet attempts to force a crossing over the Luchesa. In the following days, the enemy sought to increase the striking power of his assaults. After a one-hour heavy barrage, he commenced his attack on 9 February along the entire sector of the 131st Infantry Division. With armoured and air support, his intention was to ruthlessly smash through the Noviki bridgehead. Even so, many of his thrusts were bloodily beaten back. He carried out a series of ten attacks of up to regimental strength against the northern wing of the division, west of Popovka, and succeeded in slightly widening the bridgehead on the west bank of the Luchesa, albeit with particularly heavy losses. Against the right wing of the 206th Infantry Division, the Soviets pushed all day long and achieved a two-kilometre-deep penetration northwest of Bondari. An immediate counterthrust of ours brought the enemy to a halt. He mercilessly threw ever more troops into battle, suffered heavy casualties, and expended a great deal of materiel, yet this was all utterly disproportionate to his limited gains.

10 February proved to be a very difficult day for the embattled troops of the 299th, 131st, and 206th Infantry Divisions. Nonetheless, all enemy assaults against the 299th Infantry Division and against the southern sector of the 131st Infantry Division were repelled. Only southwest of Popovka did the Soviets manage, on this day as well as on 11 February, to expand their bridgehead over the Luchesa. In the central sector of the 206th Infantry Division, they advanced on either side of Bondari.

On the afternoon of 12 February, the enemy once more struck the Noviki bridgehead. This time he was supported by artillery, flame throwers, armour, and ground-attack aircraft. He also pushed towards the west from his own bridgehead southwest of Popovka. We were able to deal with the latter, but the Soviets, despite our fierce resistance, broke through the southern and eastern fronts of the Noviki bridgehead. The brave garrison there had repelled 33 enemy assaults and had destroyed 10 tanks since 3 February. Lance Corporal Fuchs from the 131st Artillery Regiment had displayed considerable cool-headedness in this fighting. With his light field howitzer, he scored direct hits against nine enemy tanks, putting them all out of action. The heavy fighting of the last couple of days was acknowledged in the daily Wehrmacht communique, with both the Lower Saxon 131st Infantry Division under the leadership of Major-General Friedrich Weber and the East Prussian 206th Infantry Division under Lieutenant-General Alfons Hitter being mentioned. Also mentioned on 13 February was the outstanding performance of the 529th Grenadier Regiment under Lieutenant-Colonel Heinrich Kiesling, a recipient of the Knight's Cross of the Iron Cross with Oak Leaves, and of the 299th Artillery Regiment under Lieutenant-Colonel Reinking.

In the next few days, the garrison in the Noviki bridgehead, which was by now split in two and significantly weakened, held out in turbulent combat against all enemy attempts to hurl them over the river. At the bridgehead southwest of Popovka – the establishment of which had required five rifle divisions as well as two refreshed divisions from the reserve of the 33rd Army – the enemy achieved little success aside from some minor territorial gain.

According to the statements provided by Soviet prisoners, we had inflicted upon the enemy so high a death toll that neither the late arrival of an armoured brigade nor the combined efforts of his remaining rifle divisions could compensate for his ever-weaker striking power. Although he conducted a few feeble attacks along the Luchesa front, the fighting in the vicinity southeast of Vitebsk come to a temporary end on 17 February. During this 14-day battle in the sector of the VI Corps, which was led by General of the Infantry Hans Jordan, the enemy had also twice sought, with his 5th Army, to overcome the German defence on the southern side of the breakthrough area.

Defensive combat northwest of Vitebsk (Map 15)

At the same time as the Soviet armies southeast of Vitebsk had commenced their attack on 3 February, the 11th Guards Army and the bulk of the 4th Shock Army to the northwest of the city had launched their decisive advance on either side of Lake Zaronovskoye in the Bondarevo–Gorbachi sector. He pushed forward following a two-and-a-half-hour heavy barrage of more than 40,000 rounds. Fighting with ever increasing ferocity, he continued his assault in the afternoon further north and south of the lake. With strong air support, he had, by the end of the day, advanced 3 to 4 kilometres along an 11-kilometre stretch of the front. In the late afternoon, enemy forces, including approximately 20 tanks, lunged through the weak central sector of the 12th Infantry Division. By the evening, we were unable, despite our rapid countermeasures, to close the gap that had opened up here. On this day, elements of the 18th Flak Division, which was employed in the area of the Third Panzer Army, shot down eleven enemy ground-attack aircraft.

The Soviets exploited their success of the first day by carrying out night raids and then pushing further forward on 4 February, thereby giving the troops of the 20th Panzer Division and of the 12th Infantry Division no chance to rest. We were unable to regain the ground that we had relinquished since the previous evening. Only after defending against numerous attacks could a new line of resistance be set up. This line ran from northeast of Bondarevo, through Kosly and Bolshaya Rubiny, and along the north bank of the stream leading to Gorbachi. But even this line had become riddled with holes by nightfall.

We had to draw on additional forces, amongst them several armoured units, both from the northwest and from the vicinity to the east of Gorodok, although this only aided the Soviet onslaught. We suffered heavy losses and were compelled to withdraw, but we made it as difficult for the enemy as we possibly could. He pierced the front on the boundary between the 20th Panzer Division and the 12th Infantry

Division. From here, Soviet forces drove eastward and southward, the result being that Bolshaya Rubiny and Stepankova fell into his hands. In a rapid counterattack by the 279th Grenadier Regiment as well as by tanks and assault guns, the enemy was thrown back, Bolshaya Rubiny was retaken, and the frontline was re-established. Elements of the 95th Infantry Division that had arrived in the meantime were used by the LIII Corps to strengthen the front.

The line of attack of both of the Soviet armies that had been carrying out their offensive from the northwest, as had been evident from the course of the fighting thus far, was directed along either side of the highway towards Vitebsk. Even so, just as was the case southeast of the city, the enemy had already suffered such high casualties on the first day that, for the next couple of days, he was no longer in the position to maintain the momentum he had built up. Only on the fourth day, 6 February, was he able to renew his attack by concentrating the eight guards and four rifle divisions currently in the vicinity. His efforts were without success between the highway and Bondarevo, but he did manage, after a one-hour heavy barrage, to push forward on a four-kilometre front into the woodland southwest of Gurki. An immediate counterattack of ours intercepted this advance.

It was clear that the enemy intended to continue the offensive not only with the 2nd Guards Rifle Corps, but with all available reserves. On 9 February, after two relatively quiet days, there was an eruption of ferocious fighting on both sides of the Vitebsk road. Even though the enemy employed four rifle divisions, two tank brigades, and waves of ground-attack aircraft against a narrow sector of the front, he did not manage to smash through our lines. The 20th Panzer Division held its position, and, by committing its armour and reserves, it had regained the terrain that had been lost south of Stepankova by the late afternoon. Twenty-seven enemy tanks were destroyed. In the sector of the 12th Infantry Division, the fighting unfolded less favourably because of the dense woodland and impenetrable marshland. The right wing of the division was pushed back as Soviet armour surged forward into the woodland south and southwest of Gurki. It was in these woods that further combat took place.

On 12 February, the Soviets pressed further forward into the northern outskirts of Staroye Syalo, in the process of which they infiltrated the woods to the north and northwest of the village. A counterattack of ours from the eastern side of the village threw back the enemy forces there to the position they had occupied that morning, but we made no progress on the northwestern side.

Presumably as a result of persistent snow flurries and of high enemy casualties, the fighting abated considerably in the northern combat zone from 11 February. Since the enemy had been unable to punch through the front in a southeasterly direction towards Vitebsk, he decided to shift the point of main effort of his offensive further south with a view to reaching the bend of the Western Dvina. For days, there was intense fighting in the woods northwest of Staroye Syalo, and this extended to the northeast of the village on 16 February. The area to the northwest repeatedly changed hands in day-and-night fighting. Yet despite the fact that the enemy had had a steady flow of reinforcements since the beginning of the battle, he gained only a small amount of territory in this particular sector. The twelve assaults that the enemy had executed on 16 February between 2:15 am and 4:15 pm against the central and left sectors of the 12th Infantry Division had been a costly failure, and it was with this that the combat on the northwest front of the panzer army came to a close.

Reflection on the second defensive battle around Vitebsk (Map 16)

In the battle of materiel that had been raging since 3 February, the Soviet leadership had endeavoured, by concentrating its attacking divisions and by massing its artillery to a degree never-before seen, to break through the positions of the Third Panzer Army so as to subsequently advance along the shortest routes from the southeast and the northwest towards Vitebsk, to take Vitebsk, and to thereby annihilate a large number of German forces in the 'Vitebsk fortress'. This failed. The enemy did not even manage to cut off the main routes of supply of the panzer army – the Vitebsk–Orsha railway line to the west of the Luchesa and the Vitebsk–Lepel road to the south of the Western Dvina.

The enemy was ruthless in his use of six armies (consisting of 53 guards and rifle divisions; 1 rifle brigade; 10, or perhaps even 16, tank brigades; 2 assault-gun regiments; 1 artillery division with elements of 2 further divisions; 1 army artillery regiment; 1 guards mortar division with 8 regiments; and 2 guards combat engineer brigades), yet his territorial gain was quite small and his units lost much of their attacking power.

Southeast of the city, the divisions under the command of Jordan foiled the enemy at every step. They stood firm and caused the Soviets, especially those at the Noviki bridgehead, enormous losses in men and materiel.

On the particularly difficult terrain between Lake Losvida and the Western Dvina, the LIII Corps, temporarily under the command of Lieutenant-General John Ansat, intercepted and struck back at numerically superior enemy forces.

Nine hundred prisoners and deserters had been captured during the battle; 332 enemy tanks had been destroyed and a further 31 rendered immobile. Ninety guns, antitank guns, and mortars, as well as 266 machine guns, had been taken. Forty enemy aircraft had been shot down.

During this time, the German side had fought with 13 infantry divisions, 1 Jäger division, 1 panzer division, 17 army artillery battalions, 6 rocket projector battalions, 5 assault-gun brigades, 2 Tiger brigades, and 2 heavy antitank battalions (one of which was equipped with Hornets).

In terms of manpower, the three German corps with their 19,150 men had confronted six Soviet armies with 152,500 men. The relative strength had therefore been 1:8. This ratio had been even more unfavourable at those locations where the enemy had chosen to exert pressure. On a 30-kilometre sector of the front southeast of Vitebsk, three German divisions with 4,700 men had faced Soviet forces amounting to 48,000 men, a ratio of 1:10. Most unfavourable though had been the ratio of 1:16.5 northwest of the city. On a 25-kilometre front, two German divisions with 2,650 men had been opposed by 43,900 Soviet troops.

CHAPTER 15

Regrouping of the Third Panzer Army, and further combat on its right wing

On 17 and 18 February, north of Lake Zaronovskoye, we observed large formations of enemy infantry and artillery heading north. This suggested that the enemy had temporarily abandoned his offensive plans northwest of Vitebsk, confirmed a few days later by the appearance of the 11th Guards Army and part of the 4th Shock Army on the front before the neighbouring Sixteenth Army.

Southeast of Vitebsk, the Soviets strove in the following weeks to gain ground west of the Luchesa, but they met with no success. The 197th and 131st Infantry Divisions swapped their positions in this area on 19 February. Northwest of the city, on 16 February, the 95th Infantry Division assumed responsibility for the sector that had previously been covered by the 20th Panzer Division. The latter was subsequently detached from the panzer army. The 5th Jäger Division took over the sector of the departing 12th Infantry Division. The new Corps Detachment D, a divisional unit assembled from two divisions that had decimated in summer 1943, moved to where the 5th Jäger Division had been.

The presence of enemy activity on 21 February near the boundary between the 256th and 211th Infantry Divisions indicated that an attack might be launched there. According to POW statements, the enemy intended to drive forward from here towards the west as far as the Vitebsk–Orsha road, thereby cutting an important supply line to the panzer army. On 22 February, the Soviets moved against and penetrated the northern wing of the 252nd Infantry Division. Overnight, some enemy units infiltrated our position through thick woodland. The next day, with the support of a tank brigade, they pushed a five-kilometre sector of our front back two kilometres to the west and northwest. The strength of the enemy's attacking divisions had deteriorated during these first couple of days, but they were soon reinforced by another division. He then persisted with his efforts to push further west and northwest by conducting multiple raids over the next few days. Although we thwarted his efforts, we did not regain the territory we had lost.

At about the same time as a counterattack was taking place on 4 March, First Lieutenant Karl-Heinz Rauch, leading an assault detachment of the 256th Replacement Training Battalion, rushed the main enemy base in the northern part of the point of penetration. On his own initiative, he proceeded to seize another base in fierce close combat, thereby putting himself in a good position for carrying out more attacks. Finally, on 12 and 13 March, we conducted a counterattack and retook the terrain that we had lost. The enemy had therefore expended the fighting power of several of his rifle divisions without even achieving the slightest territorial gain.

CHAPTER 16

The removal of units from the Third Panzer Army, and the first discussion of a 'Vitebsk fortress'

On 23 February, the panzer army, from which the 20th Panzer Division had recently been transferred, received from the army group the order to release another three divisions due to the threatening development of the situation for the Ninth Army. In a meeting with Field-Marshal Busch the following morning, we managed to reach an agreement whereby only two of these divisions would be released, whilst the third would initially be kept in the panzer army reserve. We also made it clear that the frontline would have to be shortened. Busch therefore approved a withdrawal of the front to the so-called second position east, northeast, and north of Vitebsk. This would shorten the frontline by approximately 25 kilometres, thus enabling the detachment of the 131st Infantry Division and of the 6th Luftwaffe Field Division. At the same time, the 14th Infantry Division would assume responsibility for what had been the sector of the 211th Infantry Division, for the latter was to be handed over to the Ninth Army. The 6th Luftwaffe Field Division would move to the vicinity west of Vitebsk on the night of 28/29 February so that it could relieve the 5th Jäger Division, also allocated to the Ninth Army, on the frontline at the beginning of March. The 131st Infantry Division was to be put into the OKH reserve in the Ula region, and the 95th Infantry Division would be assembled in the Vitebsk–Ostrovno area from 3 April.

The crucial point in the second part of the meeting with Busch was the demand by the Führer that Vitebsk be declared a 'fortress'. A battle commandant would be assigned to the city with a defensive group that, in the event of an encirclement, was to stand to the last. We were horrified by this order. This was a case of prestige over common sense! The field-marshal stated quite frankly that three divisions of the panzer army would have to allow themselves to be encircled along with the city. It was further required that one of the corps generals be appointed as commandant of the Vitebsk fortress and that he be put under the direct command of the field-marshal. The result of this was the novelty that the commandant as a front commander would receive his orders from Reinhardt, the commander of the Third Panzer Army, until the encirclement was complete, but in matters pertaining to the Vitebsk fortress this same commandant would take orders, even now, from Busch, the commander of the army group. Reinhardt firmly pointed out that this split subordination would pose serious difficulties, yet Busch refused to be persuaded.

Reinhardt further argued that, although the three divisions might establish a defensive ring around Vitebsk, the enemy would not necessarily complete his encirclement along the boundary of this ring. He would quite likely attempt to break through to Vitebsk wherever seemed most favourable. In the south, this would probably be on the Luchesa, near Sosnovka; in the northwest, at a point on the Western Dvina where he was nearest – thus to the north of Ostrovno. This would mean the envelopment of not three but at least four-and-a-half divisions. A 40-kilometre gap would thereby open up in the front of the panzer army. How would it be closed? The panzer army would have no available forces.

The field-marshal said that this would not be our concern. The necessary forces would be made available when the time came. Reinhardt was doubtful. He was of the view that such forces would have to be on hand even before the beginning of the Soviet offensive, especially if Vitebsk were to be a stronghold following its encirclement. Busch was dismissive. He repeatedly invoked the order of the Führer. Reinhardt replied that the probable expenditure of more than three divisions and the likely development of a 40-kilometre gap, which would pose a threat to the entire panzer army, would have to be made clear to the Führer. The Soviets would pour into this gap, and the panzer army would be swept away to either side and annihilated.

Reinhardt proceeded to outline the view of the panzer army. Holding Vitebsk was not what was most important. Rather, it was crucial that the front of the panzer army and its supply lines be maintained. Given our shortage of troops, we could not afford to commit, let alone sacrifice, entire divisions on grounds of prestige. Such an effort would not even tie down any significant quantity of Soviet forces. Although the enemy would leave behind a few forces to surround Vitebsk, he would have the bulk of his troops bypass the city on either side. His objective was not to capture Vitebsk but to advance into the Baltic states. It was the recommendation of the high command of the panzer army to evacuate Vitebsk before the onset of the Soviet offensive, to let the enemy make his first thrust into a vacuum, and to set up a defensive position behind the Tiger Line. In this lake-dotted position, it would be possible to concentrate our forces for defending and counterattacking. There would still be sufficient time for us to establish ourselves firmly in this position, as it was unlikely that the enemy would launch his major offensive before summer.

Field-Marshal Busch rejected this recommendation. The Führer had issued his order, and that was that. He would himself in the next few days appoint the various fortress commandants, amongst them the commander of the LIII Corps, General Friedrich Gollwitzer. He intended to shake the hand of each commandant and would also ask for their utmost loyalty.

We were determined to take up the fight against this idea of a Vitebsk fortress. We had the opportunity on 27 and 28 February to present to the chief of staff of the army group, Lieutenant-General Hans Krebs, our opinion on the fortress and our proposal that we abandon Vitebsk upon the commencement of the Soviet attack. But, like Busch, he did not agree with us. The demands of the Führer held such sway that the army group simply viewed our recommendation as 'impossible'. The high command of the panzer army therefore sent to the army group a detailed memorandum outlining in all clarity the point of view on the Vitebsk fortress that Reinhardt had already presented to Busch in person. This memorandum concluded with the recommendation that the panzer army fall back to and entrench itself along the Tiger Line before the beginning of the Soviet offensive. All efforts were to go into the construction of this position over the course of the next few months.

CHAPTER 17

The end of the winter defensive battles, and renewed defensive combat on the Luchesa

After the fighting had subsided on the boundary between the 256th and 211th Infantry Divisions, the enemy launched a new attack in the early hours of the morning of 28 February with five rifle divisions of the 33rd Army against the Luchesa sector between Peravoz and southwest of Popovka. He briefly achieved a breakthrough over the Luchesa to the north of Peravoz, but he was soon forced back. Soviet activity on this day, as well as our ground reconnaissance on the following days, revealed that the enemy intended not only to cross the Luchesa but also to expand his control over the Vitebsk–Orsha railway line. He renewed his attack on 2 March, supported by a newly arrived guards tank brigade and several ground-attack aircraft. From the south and north of Myaklovo, as well as from his bridgehead north of Noviki, the enemy attempted to penetrate our defensive positions. He was especially keen to apply pressure against our two small Noviki bridgeheads. He broke through the front on the boundary between the 299th and 197th Infantry Divisions; along the rest of the front he was either smashed to pieces by our defensive fire or repelled in fierce close combat. The bridges that the enemy held on the Luchesa north of Noviki were destroyed by direct hits.

As a diversion, the enemy launched a surprise assault on the same day with a guards tank brigade east of Vitebsk. From lake-dotted terrain three kilometres north of the Vitebsk–Liozno road, 19 tanks headed northwest and rolled over our frontline with the goal of cutting our supply line. Yet these tanks were without infantry support, so we soon put them all out of action. Sergeant Roslin of the 14th Company of the 689th Grenadier Regiment had destroyed seven of these tanks all on his own. Just as fruitless for the enemy were his numerous diversionary thrusts on the following day on both sides of the Vitebsk–Liozno road.

Fierce fighting continued through this day, 3 March, in the Luchesa sector, where the enemy had received artillery reinforcements. His nonstop assaults, though supported by tanks and ground-attack aircraft, crumbled in the face of our unshakeable defence. Any small breakthroughs of his were cleared up by our rapid counterattacks. He had to abandon the small amount of territory he had gained on the west bank of the Luchesa (west of Myaklovo and near Volosovo). The enemy replenished two of his divisions – which had been battered over the last couple of days – by drawing on the reserve of the 33rd Army, thus creating a full rifle division and a full rifle brigade. Gathering these together with elements of nine divisions and two tank brigades, he launched an assault against the 197th Infantry Division on 4 March. From his bridgehead to the north of Noviki, he carried out no fewer than 14 attacks, all of them of battalion strength. He applied pressure against the southern part of the Noviki bridgehead, which we had held until now against innumerable attacks, and infiltrated the Volosovo position. At all other points along the front, the enemy was bloodily repelled, sometimes with cold steel. Five Stuka sorties on this day brought our embattled infantry marked relief.

On the following day, the enemy concentrated his operations on a narrow portion of the sector of the 197th Infantry Division. After strong preparatory fire, he conducted multiple thrusts against the Volosovo defensive position and against the northern part of the Noviki bridge-head, which was now exposed to enemy pressure from three sides. The forward trench of the Volosovo defensive position changed hands six times overnight, and it soon looked as though the Soviets were favourably placed to break through to the west. The fighting was utterly ferocious in both locations. Over and over, the enemy mercilessly shoved his infantry forward. More and more of them bled to death as our troops, with the outstanding support of our Tiger tanks, assault guns, antitank units, and antiaircraft batteries, doggedly held their positions. The garrison on the northern side of the Noviki bridgehead distinguished itself with heroic endurance under the leadership of Captain Leipold, commander of the 1st Battalion of the 347th Grenadier Regiment.

No further engagements took place in this sector on the following day. This phase of combat had come to an end due to the rapid erosion of the enemy units that had been fighting in this area. The heroic struggle of the Middle Rhenish 197th Infantry Division under the leadership of Lieutenant-General Eugen Wößner received a special mention in the Wehrmacht communique of 8 March.

Combat southeast of Vitebsk in the Sukhodrovka sector (Map 17)

Our ground reconnaissance in the middle of March revealed that the enemy was beginning a gradual build-up of his forces in the Sukhodrovka sector. Soviet troops arrived at Krynki, from where, on 17 and 18 March, they made several attempts to gain control of high ground near Shugayevo. On 21 March, the Soviets conducted three-quarters of an hour of preparatory fire with 40 to 50 batteries, which included mortars and rockets, in the Sasyby–Shugayevo sector, after which they struck with the 5th and 33rd Armies (six rifle divisions) and with a tank brigade (45 tanks). Their objective, according to subsequent statements from prisoners, was the south bank of the Sukhodrovka. Our troops held out in the Shugayevo area, but further to the west we had to fall back to the Starina–Sharki line in the face of relentless enemy pressure. He made particularly effective use of his assault guns and tanks to create points of penetration for his infantry. He then attacked with extraordinary ferocity on either side of the Vitebsk–Orsha road. It was clear that he wanted to punch through the front with his tanks and then follow up with further forces, many of them on trucks.

The enemy, reinforced with two units that had been withdrawn from the Luchesa front, advanced the next day along the entire Sukhodrovka front. After a half-hour heavy barrage, the enemy sent two regiments with tanks to each of Starina, which he captured, and Dribino. With the arrival of even more reinforcements, the Soviets pushed our troops back to the Buraki–Yazykovo line. Dribino had to be relinquished following bitter fighting and heavy casualties. We repelled all enemy attacks near Sharki and on either side of the main road, as our infantry here had been superbly supported by 90 fighter bombers and Stukas.

Drawing upon another two rifle divisions from the Luchesa front, the enemy attacked along the entire length of the Sukhodrovka front on 23 March in an attempt to break through to the south. He was staved off in bitter fighting. Our nine battalions – even though they received exemplary support from our artillery, assault guns, and Tigers – found it most challenging to defend against the onslaught of nine rifle divisions, one rifle brigade, and two tank brigades, for they had to do so whilst withstanding snow flurries, thaw by day, frost as low as minus ten degrees by night, occasional storms, and muddy roads.

Even on the fourth day, the enemy persisted with his attempts to smash through the front. He conducted several attacks of up to regimental strength, but the embattled troops of the 14th and 299th Infantry Divisions achieved a major defensive success. Enemy losses were high. It was only in the late afternoon that the enemy managed to penetrate the front southeast of Dribino, but we blocked his advance to the east and to the north of the bend in the river. He proceeded to strike our position a total of thirteen times before nightfall. Yet, despite his ruthless exploitation of his forces, the enemy made no further progress.

The enemy's units had lost so much of their fighting power that they were only able to carry out a handful of uncoordinated assaults on 25 March. Our troops made use of this moment of weakness to regain some of the territory that had been lost south of Dribino and near Kusmentsy, even though the enemy put up stubborn resistance.

After a three-day pause, fighting broke out again on the morning of 28 March. The enemy resumed his efforts to penetrate the front between Cherkassy and Makarova. He had at his disposal a newly-arrived rifle corps in addition to reinforced artillery (aerial photographs revealed 110 batteries and 404 guns), and he preceded his offensive with a half-hour heavy barrage. Our nine battalions now faced eleven enemy rifle divisions and one enemy rifle brigade. The Soviets mobilised everything they could to force a breakthrough. Although great demands had been made of the 14th Infantry Division, of the 299th Infantry Division, and of the elements of other divisions over the course of the last few weeks (with 1,600 casualties between 21 and 25 March), they were able to coordinate their efforts to bring the almighty advance of the enemy to a halt. He tried all day long to punch a hole in our frontline, but to no avail. By evening, all his assaults had either been swept away or were in the process of being wiped out. At no point along this sector of the front did the Soviets achieve anything, so they decided to disengage. Over the course of five days, we had repelled 25 attacks of regimental to divisional strength, 45 of battalion strength, and 35 of company strength. These failed attacks had been costly for the enemy, for he had lost 4,000 men and 49 tanks.

This breakthrough attempt had obviously been the final collective effort of an enemy who had been bled to death and whose materiel had been depleted. Vitebsk therefore remained firmly in German hands as the winter came to an end. The first precondition for a thrust into the Baltic states – the capture of Vitebsk with its road and railway junctions – had not been achieved by the Soviets despite their tremendous numerical superiority.

With the conclusion of the fighting in the Sukhodrovka sector, the enemy ceased combat activity along the entire front of the panzer army except for some minor assaults and the ordinary reconnaissance patrols.

The heavy fighting that the VI Corps had endured throughout both winter defensive battles for Vitebsk was finally recognised on 20 April when the commander of the corps, General of the Artillery Hans Jordan, received the Oak Leaves with Swords to the Knight's Cross of the Iron Cross. Jordan assumed command of the Ninth Army at the end of May. General Georg Pfeiffer was appointed the new commander of the VI Corps on 21 May.

The defensive combat of the Third Panzer Army during the last few months was again recognised by the highest command on 27 May in the following telegraph message to Colonel-General Georg-Hans Reinhardt:

> In consideration of your outstanding service and heroism, I name you as the 68th soldier of the German Wehrmacht to be awarded with the Oak Leaves with Swords to the Knight's Cross of the Iron Cross. Adolf Hitler.

This high decoration was met with delight and satisfaction throughout the panzer army. The success of the Third Panzer Army in fulfilling its winter defensive role as outlined in the Wehrmacht communique on 21 January 1944 – namely, of foiling the operational breakthrough sought by an enemy who was vastly superior in both numbers and materiel – had been the result of the heroism of the troops and of the superb art of leadership demonstrated by Reinhardt. The two-front war that had been characteristic of both winter defensive battles had placed the most considerable demands on the agility of our leadership. And it was Colonel-General Reinhardt who would always bear the ultimate responsibility for any decision to use our meagre reserves or to operate with our auxiliaries. It was he who would always act decisively to ensure that we overcame the many serious crises that arose.

Reinhardt was almost always in the heat of battle. When at the corps and divisional command posts, he would always offer an unfaltering and accurate appraisal of the prevailing situation. He would also urge his subordinate commanders to make the utmost use of the resources at their disposal. He never failed to make an impression with his humanity and with his extraordinary cool-headedness in the face of danger. He was a calming influence when he appeared on the frontline, even amidst the most difficult of crises. The troops were inspired by him, especially during his frequent visits to the forward-most trenches. It was not long before the entire front echoed the following view that had been expressed by a divisional commander: 'The defence of Vitebsk – that is Reinhardt!'

In his order of the day issued on 27 May, the colonel-general said to his soldiers: 'I proudly receive these Oak Leaves with Swords in the knowledge that this decoration bestows an honour on the entire Third Panzer Army for its successes in the most difficult winter fighting around Vitebsk. I offer my indelible gratitude to everyone in the panzer army for their contribution to our defensive struggle.'

The struggle of the Third Panzer Army against the designation of Vitebsk as a 'fortress'

The meeting in which Field-Marshal Busch demanded for the first time that Vitebsk be made a fortress has already been mentioned above. On 13 March, Führer Order No. 11 came into effect. All previous orders relating to battle commandants were cancelled and the term 'fortress commandant' was introduced. This order also declared Vitebsk a fortress. A fortress was, in the event of an encirclement, to be defended to the last, and to this end it was to be adequately manned and stockpiled. Its commandant would be directly subordinate and would swear allegiance to the commander of an army group, and he 'would demonstrate soldierly honour by exhausting all defensive possibilities'.

On 15 March, the high command of the panzer army recommended that the commander of the LIII Corps, General Friedrich Gollwitzer, be appointed as fortress commandant of Vitebsk. We also reported on this occasion that the execution of Führer Order No. 11 would lead to an encirclement of not three, but rather of four or five divisions, a situation that could only be catastrophic for the panzer army. At the end of March, the army group confirmed the appointment of Gollwitzer as commandant. The security garrison was given three divisions in addition to the two battalions that Reinhardt had previously allocated. Gollwitzer assumed his new position on 5 April, and on 7 April he shook hands with and swore loyalty to Busch in a meeting at the headquarters of the army group in Minsk.

In our view, the enemy would not make a frontal attack on Vitebsk. Rather, he would most likely approach the city from the old break-through areas, namely the southeast and the northwest. It would be necessary to withdraw to the defensive ring before the onset of the enemy advance, the point of main effort of which would presumably, given the disposition of his artillery, lie on his outer left wing. We were to delay this advance for as long as we possibly could. Should Vitebsk be encircled, the city was to be held for as long as possible. Nonessential supply troops would be evacuated from the encirclement so that they would be able to meet the emerging breakthrough by the enemy to the west. While there were several defensive positions to the east of Vitebsk, there were fewer to the west, so special atten-tion would be required there. The abandonment of the city and the withdrawal of the front to the Tiger Line would now only take place if it were ordered by the commander of the army group. Should our decreasing fighting power allow the enemy to penetrate into the centre of Vitebsk, the troops there were to resist to the last in their fortified strongholds.

At the command post of the LIII Corps, which was now also the command post of the fortress commandant of Vitebsk, and which, from the middle of April, had been relocated to the southwest part of the city, Colonel-General Reinhardt made it clear in a discussion with General Gollwitzer that, although Vitebsk might develop its own battle zone, it would be his task as the commander of the Third Panzer Army to maintain the entire front of the panzer army. It would be unacceptable to reinforce Vitebsk at the expense of the panzer army. Under no circumstances could an artificial encirclement be allowed. Moreover, everything was to be done to avoid encirclement for as long as possible. Most important would be the establishment of strong positions in those zones where it was anticipated that the enemy would apply his greatest effort – the left wing of the VI Corps, and the northwest of Vitebsk. The men and resources needed for such construction would have to come from the city.

Reinhardt expressed the view that the supply of food and munitions to the amount of 18,000 tonnes, as had been ordered, would be particularly problematic. None of it would be protected, for the city contained no bunkers. Stockpiling so much so near to the front would not only be unbearable; it would also contradict regulations. Reinhardt said that he would have to seek clarification on this matter, since he would not be permitted to make a decision on this himself.

Reinhardt concluded by remarking that he was firmly of the opinion that Vitebsk, because of its proximity to the front, ought not to have been designated a 'fortress' in the way that the cities of Minsk and Vilnius had been, both of which lay beyond the combat zone. The panzer army was going to form a coherent front. Any consequences that might arise would have to be dealt with. As much help as possible would be provided in terms of personnel and materiel. Just as Gollwitzer was responsible for holding the Vitebsk fortress, Reinhardt promised with soldierly honour that he would do all he could to maintain the entire front of the panzer army. The high command of the panzer army would once more raise the question of Vitebsk with the army group. He still hoped that any ideas of moving such a tremendous quantity of supplies to the city would run aground, especially as they had already been exposed to strong enemy fire even before the beginning of an encirclement. He and Gollwitzer agreed that the notion of a 'fortress', and the consequences associated with it, would only complicate matters.

As a result of this discussion, the panzer army sent to the army group a written summary of its reservations with regard to the Vitebsk fortress. In the view of the panzer army, holding on to an encircled city so far to the east of the frontline would produce more difficulties than operational advantages.

In a meeting with Field-Marshal Busch at the headquarters of the panzer army on 21 April, Colonel-General Reinhardt again objected to the designation of Vitebsk as a fortress. Holding on to the city would be of little use against the major Soviet offensive that was to be expected.

The field-marshal replied: 'Vitebsk shall retain its status as a fortress, and under no circumstances will the Führer relinquish it. He is adamant that the city will tie down thirty to forty enemy divisions that would otherwise be free to drive towards the west and southwest.'

'This fortress only makes sense,' responded Reinhardt, 'if it can be relieved by the panzer army at a later stage, but there is no guarantee that this will be the case.'

Busch: 'It is also about prestige. Vitebsk is the only place on the Eastern Front whose loss will be noticed the world over.'

Reinhardt: 'Vitebsk on its own will not tie down considerable enemy forces. The threat posed by the enemy can only be dealt with by the panzer army in its entirety. It would therefore be much better to pull everything out of the city and to hold the flanks that extend south and west. The fortress is of secondary importance.'

The field-marshal eventually agreed with the colonel-general that an encirclement of Vitebsk would not be ideal, although his army group still issued an order the following day that clearly prioritised holding on to the Vitebsk fortress over maintaining a united frontline for the panzer army. Everything would naturally be done to prevent an encirclement, but the status of the city as a fortress remained unaltered. This fortress was supposed to occupy the attention of the enemy to such an extent that our lack of units elsewhere would not be detrimental.

CHAPTER 19

Assessment of the situation in the middle of May 1944

The high command of the panzer army presented its assessment of the situation to the army group on 11 May. The enemy had withdrawn strong forces southeast of Vitebsk, and, even along the front of the Vitebsk salient, he had only a weak presence. However, the 4th Shock Army was assembling its troops for action before the left wing of the panzer army and the right wing of the Sixteenth Army. It was probable that the 11th Guards Army would also move against us in this sector. Both enemy armies would, in our view, head towards the southwest. In conjunction with an attack deep into the distant flank of the Fourth Army, the enemy would seek to envelop both the Fourth Army and the Third Panzer Army. Vitebsk would thereafter be operationally insignificant, so the enemy would not overcommit himself and be tied down there. He would instead attempt to tie us down. The focal point for the defence of the panzer army would lie not in the area of the Vitebsk fortress, but rather in that of the IX Corps. This focal point would have to be supported by drawing upon forces from other sectors of the front. We therefore requested the withdrawal of the VI Corps to the south bank of the Sukhodrovka, west of Buraki.

The authorisation for the withdrawal, which would enable the detachment of the 14th Infantry Division, was given on 24 May, and it was carried out on the night of 1 June. Although we had been repeatedly assured that the 14th Infantry Division would be kept in reserve behind the right wing of the panzer army, the army group ordered on 13 June the immediate transfer of this division to the vicinity of the Fourth Army. Now only the 95th Infantry Division was available in the panzer army reserve.

CHAPTER 20

Anti-bandit operations in the rear area of the Panzer Army

There was barely any combat activity along the front of the Third Panzer Army in the months of April and May, as well as in the first half of June. The panzer army was able to make use of this time to respond to the increasingly dangerous bandit situation that had developed to its rear. This situation would only worsen in the event of a Soviet breakthrough. Our sole supply route to the west, via Lepel, now required the use of convoys, even at night. The main bandit areas lay southeast of Lepel and between Lepel and Polotsk. In the former, we estimated that there were approximately 7,000 armed bandits; in the latter, the so-called Ushatshi territory, approximately 15,000. Beyond that, there were smaller bandit areas northeast and southwest of Lepel. These bandits were supplied by up to 200 aircraft of the Red Air Force almost every night. We were aware that there were a number of general staff officers of the Red Army in the Ushatshi bandit territory.

To eliminate the danger that these bandits presented once and for all, and in order to make our supply route navigable again at any time, a number of anti-bandit operations were conducted throughout April and May. The objective was to clear out the major bandit areas and, so as to minimise the revival of bandit activity, to occupy these areas with our security and supply troops.

Operation *Regenschauer* was carried out in the period from 11 to 17 April. Against fierce bandit resistance, the 201st Security Division cleared out the eastern part of the Ushatshi territory. Most of the bandits were thereby pushed back into the western part of the territory. With the arrival of additional forces (including the police combat group of SS-Major-General Curt von Gottberg, the 95th Infantry Division, and a number of native auxiliary units), we were then able to advance from all sides against the Ushatshi territory. Unfavourable weather conditions (mud season) made the operation particularly difficult. Having initially given ground, the bandits, under orders from their leaders on the other side of the front to stand fast at all costs, built up a well-organised defence. They fought maliciously and slowed our advance. There are no words to describe the brutish and terrible ways in which the bandits fought at this time. At first, our troops were willing to believe the bandits whenever they indicated a desire to call off fighting. However, our soldiers were invariably mowed down by machine-gun fire as they approached to take prisoners. Over and over, small bandit groups would conceal themselves in marshland and would allow our troops to pass by. They would often lie there for several hours in the mud or under the water, drawing air from an empty bottleneck. They would then attack and murder our troops from behind in the cruellest manner. Such combat methods violated all international agreements. These bandits did not fight humanely.

The bandits had been promised help by the 1st Baltic Front, the Soviet army group standing opposite the panzer army. Enemy fighters and ground-attack aircraft flew sorties over the bandit areas, whilst ground units launched relief attacks against the front northeast of Polotsk. None of this stopped our encirclement of the bandits. Their resistance gradually waned in the face of our superior weaponry. Our air force dropped 500 tonnes of bombs over the course of 1,500 sorties, contributing to the attrition and annihilation of the bandits. The leader of the operational group in the Ushatshi territory eventually ordered that all bandits in the forests in the western part be brought together so that they could break out to the west. After the failure of this combined effort, the order was issued for a breakout in small groups. While most of these smaller attempts were foiled, roughly 3,000–4,000 bandits managed to escape to the west. The vast majority of them would still be cleared out. The ascertainable losses of the bandits between 11 April and 15 May amounted to 14,288 men. Materiel captured or destroyed during this operation, which from 18 April went under the code name of *Frühlingsfest*, were an artillery piece, twelve antitank guns, 48 mortars, 42 antitank rifles, 116 machine guns, 72 submachine guns, and a large quantity of rifles, pistols, ammunition, and explosives. This demonstrates not only how heavily armed the bandits were, but also how dangerous they would have been – especially given their cruelty – in the event of a breakthrough by the Red Army into the rear of the Third Panzer Army.

In the next few weeks, all efforts by the straggling bandits to regroup were thwarted by our mopping-up operations in the woodlands of the Ushatshi territory. Several hundred of these bandits were rendered harmless.

After the success of Operation *Frühlingsfest*, the bandits in the area southeast of Lepel fell back towards the west. Nonetheless, the VI Corps, in Operation *Pfingstausflug*, encircled and annihilated some of them in the western half of the area. Two more successful operations, one southeast and the other northeast of Lepel, took place in the first few days of June. The bandits that had escaped or had been pushed to the southwest were subsequently obliterated under the leadership of the army group.

These operations resulted in a marked reduction in the threat posed by the bandits. Their disruptive activity, particularly the laying mines, diminished almost completely. This achievement of ours was of decisive importance for the overall situation on the boundary between the two army groups.

CHAPTER 21

The Soviet summer offensive of 1944: the advance against the Third Panzer Army

In the second half of May, after an almost two-month break from fighting, there were signs that the enemy was about to renew his efforts, already twice frustrated, to penetrate the front. Enemy reinforcements southeast of Vitebsk far exceeded what we had previously observed. Motorised and infantry movements had been revived since the beginning of June on all roads of approach. It seemed that his point of main effort would be in the Sukhodrovka sector. Traffic had increased considerably along the Smolensk–Krynki and also occasionally along the Nevel–Gorodok railway lines.

East of Vitebsk, the 5th Guards Rifle Corps of the 39th Army was shifted from its position south of the Smolensk road to the area northwest of Dribino, while the 5th Army concentrated its troops in the Sukhodrovka sector. Northwest of Vitebsk, the 43rd Army moved towards Lake Zaronovskoye. The enemy covered the rest of the front that swept around the city with just five rifle divisions and a fortification zone. There was a significant build-up of Soviet artillery before the IX Corps, and they would no doubt be followed by strong infantry forces.

There could be no mistake that the enemy was making preparations on both sides of Vitebsk. The high command of the panzer army had already predicted this development in its assessment of the situation on 11 May.

We suspected at this time that another guards army was on its way. According to the information we had gathered from spies and POWs, a new army headquarters had been set up in the vicinity of Liozno and, furthermore, guards troops from Crimea were flowing into the area southeast of Vitebsk. The Soviets sought to mask this assembly of troops by using camouflage and by reducing headquarters radio traffic. Aerial photographs provided evidence that fresh Soviet troops were arriving by rail. Thereafter, at least 13 divisions appeared in the area between 28 May and 14 June. We failed to detect the movement of the 5th Guards Tank Army, which the enemy had restored to full strength near Smolensk, to the area southeast of Vitebsk at the beginning of June. However, we did spot the 11th Guards Army as it came close to the boundary with the Fourth Army. On the left wing of the panzer army, where Soviet artillery was by now in position, the 6th Guards Army drew near and prepared itself to thrust south or southwest.

Altogether, the enemy had a significant quantity of forces at his disposal. Southeast of Vitebsk were the 5th and 39th Armies with 18 to 20 rifle divisions, the 5th Guards Tank Army with two tank corps and one mechanised corps, and three to four tank brigades. Northwest of the city was the bulk of the 43rd Army, the 6th Guards Army with eight rifle divisions, elements of the 4th Shock Army, one tank corps, two tank brigades, and one mechanised brigade.

There was also the corresponding build-up of artillery. Southeast of Vitebsk was the 5th Artillery Corps, and our aerial reconnaissance revealed that in the Sukhodrovka sector alone there were 130 batteries with 480 guns. Northwest of Vitebsk, in addition to divisional artillery, there were at least one guards artillery brigade and three army artillery regiments (predominantly heavy artillery).

Our own forces before the beginning of the Soviet offensive

For the defence against the Soviet onslaught, the Third Panzer Army had available the forces as outlined below.

Against the anticipated thrust from the area southeast of Vitebsk, on a 65-kilometre-wide front, we had the VI Corps with the 256th, 299th, and 197th Infantry Divisions with a total of 7,038 men, i.e. 110 men per kilometre. The corps also included two assault-gun battalions, one heavy artillery battalion, and one infantry battalion for special use.

Holding the 87.5-kilometre front of the Vitebsk salient and earmarked for encirclement was the LIII Corps with the 206th Infantry Division, the 6th Luftwaffe Field Division, the 4th Luftwaffe Field Division, and the 246th Infantry Division. These divisions had a combined total of 8123 men, i.e. 94 men per kilometre. There also one heavy artillery battalion, two heavy antitank companies, and one Luftwaffe battalion for special use.

Against the anticipated thrust from the area northwest of Vitebsk, on a 64-kilometre-wide front, was the IX Corps with Corps Detachment D and the 252nd Infantry Division. Together, they had 6,462 men, i.e. 102 men per kilometre. In addition, there were one heavy battery, one heavy antitank company, and one field penal battalion.

In panzer army reserve were the 95th Infantry Division, the panzer army assault battalion, one Hornet battalion, one assault-gun brigade, one heavy artillery battalion (minus one battery), one motorised pioneer battalion, and one motorised bridge construction battalion.

The 14th Infantry Division was *in army group reserve* and was situated on the boundary with the Fourth Army.

In the rear area of the panzer army, we had the 201st Security Division and the 480th Security Battalion.

It can be seen that the panzer army had to await the Soviet summer offensive with substantially weaker forces, especially in artillery and in armour-piercing weapons, than it had possessed during the two winter defensive battles.

The first signs that the summer offensive was about to commence (Map 18)

Despite the camouflage measures taken by the enemy, it was apparent from the middle of June that he had completed preparations for a major offensive on both sides of Vitebsk. We expected the offensive to begin on 22 June, the third anniversary of our invasion of the Soviet Union.

These days were filled with far greater suspense than we had felt in the lead-up to each of the major winter defensive battles. We were aware that the summer offensive would determine the outcome of the war, one way or another. Our troops were confident as a result of our defensive successes to date, although they were by now reporting an improvement in Soviet morale since the winter battles. Recently, the enemy was fighting with the utmost tenacity, was attacking even without tanks, and was defending every single position he gained to the last.

The multiple enemy assaults at several points along the front between 17 and 21 June obviously served the purpose of conducting reconnaissance and of creating jumping-off positions for the imminent major offensive. Indeed, in the sector of the VI Corps, the enemy managed to push back the right wing of the 299th Infantry Division and to carve out a bridgehead almost five kilometres in width on the south bank of the Sukhodrovka.

The first few days of combat northwest of Vitebsk (Map 19)

The Soviets initiated their major summer offensive early in the morning of 22 June with a heavy barrage on the positions of the IX Corps. Seven or eight divisions of the 43rd Army, as well as one division of the 6th Guards Army, then struck the central and right sectors of the 252nd Infantry Division. They received support not only from two tank brigades but also from more ground-attack aircraft than we had ever previously encountered. Our bitter fighting and numerous counterthrusts enabled us to hold on to Sirotino throughout the day. Only in the evening was the enemy able to enter the village. On either side of the Obol, after some fierce seesaw combat, the enemy advanced five kilometres along an eight-kilometre sector of the front that had been occupied only by a handful of strongpoints. At Sirotino, the enemy carried out a series of relentless night assaults which pushed us back even further. He pressed the attack the following morning and cut through the Polotsk–Vitebsk railway line towards the south and southeast.

The action soon spread out. Not only did the enemy exploit his numerical superiority in men and materiel (particularly artillery and tanks); he also used his air force to murderous effect. It made much more difficult the desperate struggle of our troops, it appreciably hindered all movements near the front as well as in the rear areas, and it almost rendered impossible our aerial reconnaissance. Never before had the enemy concentrated his forces in so narrow a space as he did on 23 June. Many of our combat groups were rapidly outflanked. Our troops in the lake-dotted region of the Tiger Line often found themselves attacked from two sides by waves of Soviet infantry and armour. They defended doggedly whilst thunderstorms appeared over the battlefield, but, by the afternoon, they had been forced back to a position west of Shumilino. On both sides of the Obol, the enemy pushed the 24th Infantry Division, which had only just the previous evening been put under the command of the panzer army and placed on the left wing of the 252nd Infantry Division, approximately three kilometres from the Tiger Line towards the southwest.

The consequences of this disappointing day quickly unfolded during the night. We had lost and were unable to regain the lake territory of the Tiger Line. The Soviets had broken through this line and were hastening the isolation of Vitebsk by lunging towards the southwest, the south, and, most ominously, the southeast. By the evening, they had reached the observation line eight to ten kilometres north of Beshenkovichi, the location of the headquarters of the panzer army. We decided that the IX Corps should withdraw overnight to a position behind the Western Dvina, and that it should hold this position. The observation line would still be defended in the meantime, so that a connection could be established between it and the Marder defensive line south of the Western Dvina, where security troops were to be placed.

The headquarters of the panzer army was temporarily shifted to Bocheikovo on the morning of 24 June. By the evening, it had relocated to Borovka (see Map 20), from where signal communications could be better guaranteed.

Heavy fighting lasted throughout the night of 23/24 June. The enemy pierced the front at several points, but the IX Corps maintained its position along the Western Dvina throughout the morning. All available standby and construction units were engaged in combat, and the

505th Pioneer Battalion under the leadership of Captain Eberhard Wolff acquitted itself particularly well against overwhelmingly superior enemy forces. An endless line of supply wagons flowed back from Vitebsk along the only road that remained open: Beshenkovichi–Bocheikovo–Lepel. They, as well as our combat troops, were unremittingly targeted by Soviet fighter-bombers.

The first few days of combat southeast of Vitebsk (Map 18)

Since 22 June, the situation in the combat zone of the VI Corps had developed even more unfavourably, indeed even more catastrophically, than that in the combat zone northwest of Vitebsk.

On the morning of 22 June, we formed, in heavy fighting, an interdiction front on the right wing of the 299th Infantry Division, i.e. against the point of penetration that the enemy had chosen the previous day. In the early afternoon, after some brief yet intense preparatory fire, the Soviet 5th Army started its advance with at least four tank brigades against the left wing of the 256th Infantry Division, and against the entire sector of the 299th Infantry Division. Powerful infantry and armoured forces managed to drive forward in three locations. The fighting lasted well into the evening, in the course of which an 18-kilometre sector of our now rather disconnected front was pushed back by two to six kilometres. The enemy also broke through the right wing of the 197th Infantry Division in the late afternoon. Our own front was thereby thrown back four kilometres to the west bank of the Luchesa. In order to improve the chances of the VI Corps for the following day, we decided to reinforce it with a regiment of the 95th Infantry Division and with armour-piercing weapons.

We were disappointed with how grave the situation had become both to the northwest and to the southeast of Vitebsk, and only one day had passed. We awaited the next day with trepidation.

The fighting to the southeast of the city lasted throughout the night and continued well into the following day. The enemy lay down the strongest fire from mortars, heavy infantry weapons, artillery, and automatic guns, and he also ensured the close coordination of his tanks and ground-attack aircraft. With such tremendous force, he was able to charge further towards the south and southwest. On either side of the Vitebsk–Orsha road, the Soviets crossed and proceeded beyond the Luchesa. On the right wing of the 197th Infantry Division, the enemy conducted a heavy barrage and then threw at us the recently arrived 5th Guards Rifle Corps. Both here and along the entire front of the 299th Infantry Division, the enemy inflicted severe losses upon our struggling troops and pushed them back some distance. Several regiments of the 95th Infantry Division launched counterattacks, but they made no impression against the superior strength of the Soviet onslaught. The bulk of the 39th Army ploughed through the front towards the west with the objective of circling to the northwest and enveloping Vitebsk. Its spearheads crossed the Vitebsk–Bogushevsk road near Shilki on the evening of 23 June. Our small combat groups on the left wing of the 299th Infantry Division and on the right wing of the 197th Infantry Division were unable to stem the tide of enemy troops. The Soviet breakthrough between the VI and LIII Corps had been executed successfully. Roughly half of the 197th Division was separated from the VI Corps and, as had been feared by the headquarters of the panzer army, was pushed back into the area of the LIII Corps. We had no more reserves upon which we could draw for intercepting the enemy. Only the 95th Infantry Division, which was on the left wing of the VI Corps, stood its ground.

In order to re-establish a coherent front for the VI Corps, we ordered a riposte in the Babinovichi–Moshkany sector (i.e. behind the Luchesa and Obolyanka Rivers) for the night of 23/24 June.

There was a dispute in the early evening between Field-Marshal Busch, who had spent the day with the IX Corps, and Colonel-General Reinhardt, for the latter spoke of the lack of timely assistance. The field-marshal categorically rejected Reinhardt's repeated proposal that Vitebsk be evacuated. Reinhardt then suggested a small withdrawal of the as-yet unscathed LIII Corps, a measure that would economise on forces defending the Vitebsk pocket. Busch dismissed this recommendation at first, but he eventually agreed to pass it on to the OKH. We received the necessary authorisation that very evening. As a part of this withdrawal, the 4th Luftwaffe Field Division was detached from the front and was dispatched to the area southwest of Vitebsk. It was to set up a westward-facing defence and, if need be, would strike towards the south.

As was the case northwest of Vitebsk, events unfolded rapidly to the south and southwest of the city on 24 June. Enemy infantry and tanks punched through the newly-created Luchesa–Obolyanka line in the morning. Meanwhile, the 14th Infantry Division, which had just been placed under the command of the VI Corps, was sent to cover the lake-dotted sector of the Tiger Line on either side of Bogushevsk. The division was soon overrun, with both sides suffering heavy casualties. Soviet tanks infiltrated Bogushevsk in the afternoon and, in the absence of any serious resistance, proceeded to advance further south and southwest. This advance by the 5th Army was clearly connected with the enemy operation on the highway near Orsha, for both were directed towards the southwest. This had already been predicted by the headquarters of the panzer army in its appraisal of the situation on 11 May.

The enemy also pierced the Tiger Line near Khodtsy, where there were more lakes and where the rest of the 197th Infantry Division was located, together with some standby units. Sweeping aside what little resistance we could offer, the Soviets drove further to the west and to the southwest. Meanwhile, another Soviet spearhead enveloped the left wing of the VI Corps by thrusting westward near Stanki and then gradually veering towards Senno. By hastily gathering together some forces here, we briefly delayed the advance of the enemy into the rear of the corps.

Throughout the afternoon, elements of the 39th Army flowed through the gap that had opened up between the VI and LIII Corps. They advanced towards the northwest as far as Ostrovno and towards the west. They had reached the Western Dvina near and to the east of Pushkari by the evening. The LIII Corps was thereby peeled away from the front of the panzer army and was finally encircled. There was an immense gap of 35 to 40 kilometres between the VI and IX Corps. Later that evening, the enemy applied further pressure against the Tiger

Line, which by this point was only defended with standby units to the south of the Western Dvina.

The headquarters of the Third Panzer Army continues to urge an evacuation of Vitebsk

Early on the morning of 24 June, the chief of the general staff of the army, Colonel-General Kurt Zeitzler, having travelled from Führer Headquarters in Berlin, was staying at the headquarters of Army Group Centre in Minsk. He wanted full details of the catastrophic development of the situation in the Vitebsk sector so he could report to the Führer, who at that point in time was on the Obersalzberg. At 3:20 pm, Zeitzler, who had by now returned to the Obersalzberg, telephoned Colonel-General Reinhardt and asked whether he regarded the evacuation of Vitebsk as essential. Reinhardt gave a brief description of the current situation: 'There is already a loose encirclement around the LIII Corps. This is the last chance we will have for ordering a breakout. The noose to the west of Vitebsk is being drawn tighter with every passing minute.' In response, Zeitzler said that the Führer had reservations about ordering such a breakout, as he thought it would cause our supplies and ammunition to dwindle away. 'A breakout must be ordered at once!' countered Reinhardt. 'The encirclement will result not only in the loss of ammunition and food supplies but also of the entire LIII Corps with its five divisions.'

'Please stay on the line,' said Zeitzler. 'I will go to the Führer again.'

There was a wait of several dreadful minutes. Three, four, five minutes! The commander of the Third Panzer Army, who had been celebrated for almost four months in all of the German daily papers as the 'victor of Vitebsk', was now striving for the one decision that had to be taken: the abandonment of a city that had for so long been so contested. These five minutes seemed like an eternity. We, and perhaps we alone, directly involved as we were in what was taking place, knew that every passing minute could cost the lives of our soldiers. Even the existence of an entire corps was at stake. Finally, at 3:28 pm, Zeitzler returned to the phone: 'The Führer has decided that Vitebsk is to be held.'

We were thunderstruck by this incomprehensible decision. What now? What hope was there? It was not long before we received a radio message from the commandant of Vitebsk, General Friedrich Gollwitzer. He reported that the enemy had taken two villages directly to the south of Ostrovno, thereby rendering unusable the road leading from Vitebsk to the west. This message had unfortunately arrived a minute too late, but Reinhardt passed it on straight away to the chief of staff of Army Group Centre, Lieutenant-General Hans Krebs, with the urgent request that it be given to Zeitzler. It was hoped that the Führer would then change his mind.

At 4:10 pm, there was a new radio message from Vitebsk: 'Immediate decision requested. Ostrovno has in the meantime been captured, so Vitebsk is practically encircled.'

At 4:11 pm, Krebs conveyed the news that the Führer stood by his decision and that he was ordering the Third Panzer Army to assign the forces that had left Ostrovno the task of reopening, and keeping open, the road leading west from Vitebsk. Krebs added that Field-Marshal Busch would, in one hour's time, ask the Führer to alter his decision. Until then, the order to hold Vitebsk would stand.

At 4:40 pm, a radio message was sent to Gollwitzer with the order that the city was still to be held. A tighter ring would be formed around Vitebsk so that a division would be made free to reopen the road to the west.

For two nerve-racking hours, we waited for a new decision to be made. The longer we waited, the more convinced we became that it would have to be made in our favour, i.e. that we would finally be permitted to abandon Vitebsk. Yet the decision that was eventually taken turned out to be more incomprehensible than the last. It arrived at approximately 6:30 pm: 'The LIII Corps will fight its way through to the west and to our own lines, but it is to leave behind one division as an occupying force in Vitebsk. The name of the divisional commander is to be reported. He will be sworn in over the radio as the new commandant of the Vitebsk fortress. His utmost commitment is mandatory.'

We were most surprised by this order. It would be impossible, especially in the space of a few hours, for one division to take over a task that had originally been envisaged for three divisions. Even holding the inner defensive ring would be a challenge for this one division. Its forces would be insufficient to defend the 20-kilometre circumference of the outskirts of the city. The only possibility for success lay in an immediate breakout attempt by all divisions. From hour to hour, the ring to the west of the city was being drawn ever tighter. At the same time, the front of the panzer army, or what was left of it, continued to be pushed further and further to the west of Vitebsk.

We were exhausting our resources at an alarming rate – more so than we had feared. It was for this reason that the high command of the panzer army made, in the afternoon, a final request to the Führer for a breakout by all elements of the LIII Corps. Although he had attached no value to our many warnings before the beginning of the summer offensive, and although he had given no credence to our assessment of the way in which we expected the battle on either side of Vitebsk to unfold, he would surely have to be convinced by now of the necessity of a breakout by the entire LIII Corps. It was still not too late. We knew that the corps might take a bit of a battering in an attempt to drive westwards, but we also felt certain that most of it ought to escape unscathed. Yet the Führer stood by his decision to water down the breakout force by ordering one division to remain behind. Not only would this guarantee the sacrifice of the division staying in Vitebsk; it would also, as far as we could tell, doom to failure the attempt to break out by the remaining divisions.

Reinhardt decided most reluctantly that the Führer's order would be obeyed. He hoped there was at least a slim chance that the weakened breakout force would manage to fight its way out of the encirclement. The following command was sent off over the radio: the 206th Infantry Division would defend Vitebsk to the last; the divisional commander, Lieutenant-General Alfons Hitter, would become the new commandant of the city; and the remaining units and troops of the LIII Corps were to extract themselves from the encirclement as soon as possible.

The night of 24/25 June 1944 (Maps 19 and 20)

The enemy was already carrying out multiple assaults against the new front along the Western Dvina in the sector of the IX Corps in the afternoon of 24 June. He succeeded in crossing the river to the north-west of Beshenkovichi. He did the same with 15 tanks to the northeast of the town. Our plan to put a security regiment behind the Marder defensive line south of the Western Dvina was thus called into ques-tion, particularly as the enemy was also feeling his way towards this position from the east. On the left wing of the corps, where parts of the newly subordinated 290th Infantry Division had recently cleared the Obol–Sludysh road, the enemy conducted heavy preparatory fire and, all day long, hurled masses of infantry and armour against our front. We repelled these attacks and inflicted significant casualties on the enemy.

Our men had to withstand a great deal on this day. The enemy lay down the most intense artillery fire, and he applied considerable pressure at several points along the front with his ground troops. In addition, he sent wave after wave of fighters and ground–attack aircraft against us. Our movements were delayed, our troops were hindered in ground combat, and almost all of our signal communications were neutralised.

On the night of 24/25 June, the Soviets widened the gap between the VI Corps and the Western Dvina, sending a steady stream of new forces into it. The embattled VI Corps was enveloped on the left wing by some of these forces and was penetrated to the south of Bogushevsk by elements of the Soviet 5th Army. The corps was placed under the command of the Fourth Army on the morning of 25 June, but its central sector, between Bogushevsk and the left wing, was smashed to pieces later that day. The Soviets had sent in the 5th Guards Tank Army from the area southeast of Vitebsk. It plunged southwestwards through the gap in the front into the area of the Fourth Army via Senno, but it avoided the rear of the Third Panzer Army for the time being. This thrust by Soviet armoured forces resulted in the VI Corps being totally cut off from the panzer army. The corps was effectively wiped out over the next few days when it was overrun by enemy tanks and infantry on the Orsha–Minsk highway. After the loss of two corps (the VI and the LIII), the Third Panzer Army found itself with completely exposed flanks and with only the struggling IX Corps at its disposal alongside some supply trains, some standby units, and the panzer army service school.

Early on the morning of 25 June, our aerial reconnaissance indicated that the enemy was amassing his forces along all roads leading to Senno from the east and northeast, with the intention of sending them to the southwest (the 5th Guards Tank Army) and to the west and northwest (the 39th Army). From the lake territory near Khodtsy, the 39th Army advanced to the west as well as to the northwest on Beshenkovichi. It had been necessary to abandon the Marder defensive line to the south of the Western Dvina overnight. Enemy tanks were advancing in this area along the main road leading west from Vitebsk towards Beshenkovichi. The defensive line to the north of this town was pierced in the morning by tanks and infantry. The 3rd Assault Battalion distinguished itself during the withdrawal to the south bank of the Western Dvina. Only once all our own troops had crossed the great bridge over the river (the Major Loewe Bridge, which had only been officially opened in March) did our pioneers blow up this beautiful construction.

The end of the occupation of Vitebsk (Map 18)

In response to the radio command that we issued on the evening of 24 June, the LIII Corps, without the 206th Infantry Division, had made preparations during the night to break out of the Vitebsk encirclement. The corps headquarters had shifted its command post to a position 10 kilometres southwest of the city. Lieutenant-General Hitter became the new commandant of the Vitebsk fortress at 4 am.

As I met with Reinhardt on the morning of 25 June to discuss the situation on the front, he handed me his calendar sheet and pointed to the quote of the day that was printed on it: 'If there is anything mightier than fate, it is the courage to be able to bear it without wavering.'[1]

'These words,' said the colonel-general, 'shall carry much meaning for both of us on this particularly difficult day.' We both knew that the fate

---

[1]Translator's note: These are the words of Emanuel Geibel, a 19th-century German poet and playwright.

of the encircled troops would be determined on this day. If the breakout failed, the demise of our splendid panzer army would be sealed. The attempt had to be made on this day; otherwise, our front would be pushed too far to the west and out of reach for the LIII Corps.

Around noon, we sent a radio message to the corps. We anticipated that the greatest enemy resistance would be encountered should the corps try to head in a westerly direction, i.e. along the main road. In our view, more promising would be a line of attack towards the southwest or perhaps a sudden change of direction through the lakes near Khodtsy.

There was a report from the corps headquarters at 1:12 pm. 'The situation has fundamentally changed. The enemy is constantly reinforcing the ring of encirclement and is beginning to infiltrate the city of Vitebsk. The 4th Luftwaffe Field Division exists no more. The 246th Infantry Division and the 6th Luftwaffe Field Division are engaged in bitter combat on multiple fronts.'

At 3 pm, the corps reported that it had moved its command post back to Vitebsk. It also emphasised the ever-worsening situation, for enemy troops were entering the city centre.

There were many telephone conversations between Colonel-General Reinhardt and Field-Marshal Busch that afternoon. Reinhardt spoke of the uselessness of sacrificing 35,000 men; Busch said that, on the order of the Führer, Reinhardt was to have a general staff officer parachuted into Vitebsk during the night to obtain an overview of the situation from General Gollwitzer, and to remind Lieutenant-General Hitter to defend the fortress to the last. Reinhardt was outraged. With a tragedy in the offing, it was utterly ridiculous to personally present to the commandant the very same order that had been issued over the radio the previous day. It would show the greatest distrust towards a commander whose fate would be in the hands of the enemy. Also, the staff officer in question would be unable to return from Vitebsk. Reinhardt refused to sacrifice even one more soldier in the city, no matter who it was. The field-marshal pointed out that it was an express order from the Führer and that it would have to be carried out. Reinhardt was required to select an officer and to report their take-off time.

Following the 6:30 pm radio message of the previous day, in which the order to break out of the encirclement without the 206th Infantry Division had been given, there came on this day at 6:33 pm a new message with which we could, for once, agree: 'The overall situation demands that the breakout forces charge towards the southwest. They will begin at 5 am. Aerial defence will be provided in the region south-west of Vitebsk.' The high command of the panzer army radioed its approval of this decision, but Reinhardt rejected the demand that Hitter be given a repeated order in person. He telephoned Busch that evening: 'Tell the Führer that I refuse to have a general staff officer or any other soldier parachuted into Vitebsk. It is because of the Führer's demand that I have now, most unwillingly, reminded Lieutenant-General Hitter over the radio of the order to stand.' There was silence on the line for a moment or two before Colonel-General Reinhardt continued: 'Herr Field-Marshal, please also inform the Führer that if he still insists on an officer being selected to parachute into Vitebsk, there is only one in the Third Panzer Army who can be considered, and that is the commanding officer. I stand ready to carry out this mission.' An hour later, Field-Marshal Busch told Reinhardt that the Führer had reversed his decision to have a staff officer sent to the city.

At 7:30 pm, we received the following radio message from Vitebsk: 'Vitebsk shall be held to the last. Gollwitzer.' There was subsequently a request over the radio for supplies by air. This was fulfilled during the night, and enabled the garrison in Ostrovno (the remains of the 4th Luftwaffe Field Division) to hold its position.

On 26 June, our pilots reported that the spearhead of the LIII Corps was 10 kilometres to the southwest of Vitebsk by approximately 8:30 am. We sighed with relief. It seemed as if the breakout from the city had gone smoothly. But the worst was yet to come. The corps headquarters radioed around 9:15 am: 'The 206th Infantry Division has been pushed out of Vitebsk.' It had certainly been too much to expect that one division would be able assume responsibility for a task that had at first been envisioned for three divisions, especially within the space of 24 hours. Reinhardt was at the front. We passed on this radio message to the army group only after a couple of hours in the hope that it would give the 206th Infantry Division time to follow and make contact with the LIII Corps. Even Krebs, who received the message at the army group, seemed optimistic. However, Field-Marshal Busch issued a new radio command to the 206th Infantry Division around 12:10 pm to the effect that any elements of the division that remained in Vitebsk were to hold the city and fight to the end. The division acknowledged receipt of this order, but it turned out to be the last time we would hear from the Vitebsk pocket.

According to our aerial reconnaissance on this day, there were several groups of German troops in the area southwest of Vitebsk heading towards the west and the southwest. A number of smaller groups had clashed with the reversed front that the enemy had established between the lakes of the Tiger Line. Our pilots observed larger groups of German troops on the roads, in the villages, and in the forests 10 to 15 kilometres southwest of Vitebsk. These groups were all engaged in combat and were subjected to persistent bombing.

At 9 am on 27 June, the LIII Corps reported over the radio that it had pushed well beyond 13 kilometres southwest of Vitebsk and that it had broken through quite a few enemy positions. Enemy aircraft were causing our troops heavy casualties, and there was a serious shortage of ammunition. This was the last radio message from the corps. Our hopes for a successful breakout were dashed. Nevertheless, we still radioed the corps what we considered the most favourable line of advance. All we could do was to blindly transmit this message over and over.

On this day, in the villages and forests 15 to 20 kilometres southwest of Vitebsk, the fighting in which our divisions were embroiled drew to a close between 11 am and 12 pm. Precisely what happened is not known. It is as if fate had kindly chosen to cast a veil over the conclusion of this tragedy.

On 29 June, the Soviets proclaimed over their transmitters that the end had come for the defenders of Vitebsk. Five thousand were dead in the city. Another 20,000, despite their fierce resistance, had been overwhelmed by ground troops or had been annihilated by aerial bombing. Ten thousand had surrendered when issued an ultimatum. All of this was according to the enemy.

We held a moment's silence in memory for the defenders of Vitebsk when we heard this news. How could we even bear this memory? Perhaps we could do so because we had only a very short time in which to think about it. Everything had happened in quick succession over the past few days, and our commanders still had to put in the greatest effort to save as much as possible.

The fighting withdrawal in the Beshenkovichi–Lepel–Berezina area (Map 20, later Map 1)

The situation confronted by the panzer army worsened from hour to hour on 25 June. During the preceding night and in the course of the day, the Soviets gradually widened the already huge gap between the VI Corps and the Western Dvina, allowing strong forces to advance westwards unchecked. Beshenkovichi was encircled in the morning. The garrison there, comprised of elements of Corps Detachment D under Major-General Bernhard Pamberg, fought heroically as it bore the brunt of the assault. It bravely held its ground and prevented the enemy from crossing the river from north to south. That evening, the garrison received the order to fight its way back to our own lines overnight.

In the meantime, the 6th Guards Army had crossed the Western Dvina at several points between the embattled towns of Beshenkovichi and Ula with the recently arrived 1st Tank Corps together with two further tank brigades. A counterattack by the 252nd Infantry Division 10 kilometres northwest of Beshenkovichi made some initial headway against the enemy group that had been ferried across the river there. But then the enemy surged forward over the Beshenkovichi–Ula road towards the southwest and west. He was brought to a halt at the Svechanka, but the main road between this river and Beshenkovichi was now in his hands. Along the rest of the front of the Western Dvina, we managed to disrupt Soviet attempts to assemble his troops for crossing the river. Even though the 290th Infantry Division had only the previous day been subordinated to the panzer army and placed to the north of the Western Dvina, both it and the 24th Infantry Division were transferred to the Sixteenth Army in the evening. This meant that the Third Panzer Army, which had possessed 11 divisions a mere four days beforehand, now only had two battered divisions at its disposal: Corps Detachment D and the 252nd Infantry Division.

Relentless enemy air activity caused our troops and commanders a lot of trouble. Our movements were greatly hindered and our efforts to conduct aerial reconnaissance were made very difficult. Our pilots were only able to make sketchy and inconsistent reports on the enemy's positions. The commander of the Sixth Air Fleet, Colonel-General Robert Ritter von Greim, who on this day was at the headquarters of the panzer army, could do nothing to help. He said that the strength of the air fleet could only be rebuilt slowly.

Field-Marshal Busch expected from the panzer army a counterattack on a grand scale! But with what? The remains of our two divisions were engaged in fierce defensive combat. They hardly had anything, especially artillery. By noon, the situation along the Svechanka had become so grave that the decision had to be made to disengage the IX Corps from both this river and the Western Dvina as soon as possible. A new defensive position could then be formed in the lake territory 12 kilometres to the west (roughly to the north of Bocheikovo). According to our aerial reconnaissance, strong enemy forces were advancing from the vicinity of Senno towards the northwest, west, and southwest. In response, we created a new defensive front along the Ula River between Lakes Lukomlskoye and Polozerye composed of members of the panzer army service school, men separated from their units, supply troops, and security units. This front would be unable to cope with much enemy pressure given the lack of heavy, especially armour-piercing, weapons. Only a withdrawal of the 252nd Infantry Division to the lake territory would free up additional forces for the defensive front along the Ula. At approximately 2 pm, Reinhardt put in a request to the army group for this withdrawal, for we would not be permitted to make this decision ourselves. He pointed out that it was best for the division, under pressure from the enemy, to retreat to the lakes rather than behind the Ula, as there were no bridges that led over the river. Although at this hour, as had been the case during the hopeless struggle of the Vitebsk garrison,

Busch did not want to know about our request. The field-marshal forbade any withdrawal of the division.

In the evening, the Beshenkovichi garrison broke through to the west and made contact with our lines. After such a bad day, this was a small ray of hope.

Only 24 hours later, on the evening of 26 June, were we allowed to give the IX Corps the order to withdraw its left wing to a position between Lakes Polozerye and Usveya. Our aerial reconnaissance reported a large concentration of enemy forces before the front of Corps Detachment D on either side of the Lepel–Kamen–Vitebsk road. Our weak forces resisted as much as they could, but Bocheikovo was lost by 4 pm. We estimated that about 60 enemy tanks had broken through the front, and by evening enemy forces were flowing along the west bank of the Ula. We could expect that the enemy would launch multiple assaults the next day from the river. It would undoubtedly be his intention to thrust deep into our rear, to disrupt our attempts to construct a new line of security, to cut off our lines of communication through Lepel, and to annihilate the panzer army to the east of the town. While the left wing of the 6th Guards Army would drive westwards, the 4th Shock Army, with several rifle divisions and a tank brigade, would conduct both a frontal attack on and, from the south, an envelopment of Obol, 15 kilometres to the north of Ula. At the same time, the 43rd Army, which Hitler had believed would be tied down by the Vitebsk garrison for a long time, would be ready to send six rifle divisions and one tank brigade forward on the southern side of the Vitebsk–Beshenkovichi road with the objective of punching through the sector between Bocheikovo and Lake Lukomlskoye.

During the night of 26/27 June, the headquarters of the panzer army was shifted to Berezino. An endless column of vehicles moved along the only east–west road from Lepel towards the west via Berezino. Many of them were the supply vehicles for the divisions that had remained in Vitebsk; others belonged to a variety of rear units. The dust on the road was incredible. Traffic discipline was surprisingly good. There was naturally the occasional traffic jam, for it was hardly possible to stray from the sandy roads. I used these roads, undetected in the darkness, to go and speak with many of our soldiers. All of them understood what was happening. Yet amongst none of them was there a hint of discontent, revolt, despair, or depression. I always heard the words: 'Reinhardt will manage it.' Some had seen the commander of the panzer army driving past at dusk. 'The colonel-general is already at his new command post,' they said, 'and he will soon be able to regain everything.' Their belief in their old commander was unwavering.

We were now most thankful that the bandit territories had been cleared prior to the onset of the summer offensive, as we now had to retreat through the swampy and wooded terrain that they had occupied. Such terrain had proven disastrous for Napoleon's troops, so even the smallest bandit units would have made our withdrawal impossible. But our men moved westwards without interruption. We saved valuable materiel and all our supply vehicles.

Two assault-gun batteries finally arrived on this evening, so we were now able to place armour-piercing weapons on either side of the line of retreat.

27 June was a much more beautiful, and far warmer, day. The only area in which trouble reigned was that of the 252nd Infantry Division, as the lake territory south of Lake Usveya was lost on this day. There was otherwise a certain easing of tension along the new defensive line that had been established overnight. This allowed us a little time to bring the 212th Infantry Division, only just put under the command of the panzer army, up to the front. Our night-time disengagement had undoubtedly compelled the enemy to reassemble his troops for the anticipated attack against the IX Corps.

We were to suffer disappointment in the afternoon, although it had not at all been unexpected. Although the combat group of Colonel Constantin Baron Digeon von Monteton (the commander of the panzer army service school) had swiftly dealt with several enemy assaults in the morning, the Soviets broke through the front to the southwest and west of Chashniki in the afternoon and advanced approximately five kilometres. A counterattack by the combat group achieved nothing, so its last reserves had to put together a defensive position 12 kilometres to the west of the front. This position lacked any form of cover on the flanks.

On the southern wing of the IX Corps, parts of the 201st Security Division were approaching to strengthen the defence there. However, the Soviets advanced five kilometres on a wide front on the southern side of the main road before the security division arrived. The enemy also managed a breakthrough on the northern side of the road. Most critical was the situation on the northern wing of the 252nd Infantry Division, where the enemy was weaving his way rapidly through the many lakes south of Lake Usveya in the early morning. We sought to block the enemy at multiple points around the lakes, but by evening it was becoming apparent that our efforts were in vain. Aerial reconnaissance spotted an enemy column advancing southwards from the southern end of Lake Tetcha at 7:40 pm. The refusal of the army group on 25 June to permit a withdrawal of the 252nd Infantry Division to this area now came back to haunt us, for the division had been severely weakened. Without any bridges over the Ula, our men had been obliged to swim naked across the river. Some of them drowned. Most of the division went barefoot. It was these circumstances that prevented us from having sufficient forces available to cover the lake territory.

During the afternoon and evening, our ground and aerial observation identified enemy formations on the roads from Bocheikovo and Ula leading towards Kamen and on the road from Ula leading towards the west. We could therefore count on a continuation of the enemy offensive on the following day. He would also push forward with the breakthrough near Chashniki, where elements of the 43rd Army had just arrived.

Reinhardt had a serious argument with Busch late that afternoon. The field-marshal wanted to split the 212th Infantry Division between the northern and southern sectors of our front. Reinhardt rejected this as a half measure. He believed that the division was needed more urgently on the northern sector. It was not long before he convinced Busch to agree with him, but the way in which events unfolded shortly thereafter meant that the division had to be moved to the Lepel region. Its task there was to prevent the panzer army from being cut off from its route of retreat.

So, against two triumphant Soviet armies, the Third Panzer Army possessed on the following morning the remaining fragments of two divisions, the still approaching 212th Infantry Division, some security troops, some stragglers who had been gathered together after escaping from the Vitebsk pocket, and a mere 70 artillery pieces (although there were many more captured guns).

28 June began in earnest. During the night, the Soviets had overrun our weak defensive line west of Chashniki whilst a simultaneous thrust had bypassed its southern flank. By the early morning, enemy troops were infiltrating Lepel from the east and south. Further north, the enemy advanced against the right wing of the IX Corps. There were a few spots where our worn-out troops managed to repel enemy attacks, supported by tanks, of up to regimental strength. The enemy suffered heavy losses as a result. Overall, though, our front lost a sense of coherency. Most of our forces were routed, with those in the Lepel region being pushed far to the southwest and with parts of the 252nd Infantry Division being pushed north into the area of the neighbouring Sixteenth Army.

Near Lepel, the 320th Grenadier Regiment, almost without any of its artillery and heavy weapons, repelled an attack by overwhelmingly superior enemy forces over the Essa to the northwest. However, there were substantial German casualties. The situation had become particularly dangerous owing to the completely open flank southwest of Lepel. We were increasingly concerned about the advance of enemy tanks and motorised infantry along both roads that led through the marshland southwest of Lepel deep into the right flank of the panzer army. These forces were stopped at the Berezina, for the bridges over the river had been destroyed, but it was possible that they would turn north and strike the rear of the 212th Infantry Division at any moment. South of Berezino, the 62nd Pioneer Battalion (motorised) barred the road leading northwards through the marshland.

A key position had been reached by the Soviets. Whilst the 5th Guards Tank Army drove southwest past Lepel into the gap between the Third Panzer Army and the Fourth Army and in the direction of Minsk, the 1st Tank Corps (from the 6th Guards Army) turned to the northwest, advanced towards the Polotsk–Drissa sector, and crossed the railway line that led southwest from Polotsk. These Soviet formations were followed by the 43rd and 39th Armies. The separation of what was left of the panzer army from the rest of the front was in the offing.

Our aerial reconnaissance revealed that 25 enemy tanks had crossed one of the two bridges west of Lepel over the Essa. We had lost our chance to destroy these bridges. The remains of the two divisions of the IX Corps reached the line running from Lake Voron to the northern side of Ushatshi. These divisions had been hotly pursued by the enemy. Our overfatigued men would be unable to withstand another attack. The 12-kilometre gap to the right wing of the Sixteenth Army could not be closed.

We could no longer speak of having an army or a front. All we had were the battle-weary and disjointed remnants of divisions, supply units, standby units, and units of the Todt Organisation. Despite this, we received an operational order from the Führer which demanded that the line running from Lepel through Kamen to the lakes further north was to be held. This order was far too late. The overall situation had fundamentally changed. The Soviets had pressed forward without resistance on the southern side of our route of retreat to the Berezina. We had absolutely nothing with which to prevent a northward thrust by the enemy into the rear of those elements of the panzer army still on the eastern side of the river. The only reasonable decision to be taken was to withdraw as quickly as possible to a position behind the river. Colonel-General Reinhardt telephoned Field-Marshal Busch in the afternoon to obtain his approval for this withdrawal. Busch gave no such approval. Reinhardt had provided a level-headed and objective appraisal of the situation, but the field-marshal responded thus: 'I've already told you that we're all under orders from the Führer – and as soldiers, we are to obey.' At midnight, Busch was relieved of his command of Army Group Centre. Over the last few months, he had borne the greatest responsibility of any commander on the Eastern Front. The constant inner conflict brought about by the demands and necessities of the front on the one hand and the opposing orders by the Führer on the other had undermined his health. He had been unable to cope with the fate that had befallen the front in the last few days.

The Third Panzer Army was no more. It had endured for two years all assaults launched against it by multiple Soviet armies. It had been victorious in the battle for Vitebsk. Its destruction had been sealed in the space of a few days by the requirements of holding Vitebsk as a fortress.

The remains of the panzer army continued to fight. They were pushed back day by day. The nearer they approached the border of East Prussia, the more doggedly they fought. It was thanks to their efforts that, after little more than three weeks, the Soviet armies were brought to a standstill at this border.

Extracts from the Wehrmacht communique, 23–29 June 1944

Over the course of the seven days of the collapse of the Third Panzer Army, the Wehrmacht communique made the following reports:

> **23 June:** The Bolsheviks have begun the attacks that we have been expecting in the central sector of the front. These attacks were conducted on a broad front with armoured and air support, but we repelled them in fierce fighting. We cleared up any small breakthroughs with immediate counterattacks. Bitter fighting is still underway on either side of Vitebsk.
>
> **24 June:** The major Soviet offensive in the central sector of the front increased in strength and stretched itself out across other sectors. Powerful infantry and armoured forces succeeded in penetrating our positions on both sides of Vitebsk. The defensive fighting here is ferocious.
>
> **25 June:** In the east, our divisions on the central sector of the front are engaged in heavy defensive combat against Soviet infantry, armour, and aircraft. The enemy made progress with a number of breakthroughs, especially in the vicinity of Vitebsk.
>
> **26 June:** In the central sector of the Eastern Front, the defensive combat continues with unabated ferocity.
>
> **27 June:** In the central sector of the Eastern Front, our courageous divisions remain engaged in heavy defensive fighting against the forces amassed by the Soviets. They have fought their way to new positions west and southwest of Vitebsk.
>
> **28 June:** Bitter fighting continues in the central sector of the Eastern Front. Following the evacuation of the cities of Orsha and Vitebsk, the defensive combat has shifted to the area east of the middle and upper Berezina.
>
> **29 June:** In the course of the bitter defensive fighting in the central sector of the Eastern Front, the Soviets have gained much territory. We continue to resist the enemy east of the middle and upper Berezina.

CHAPTER 22

Closing remarks

As described, the first few days of the Soviet summer offensive of 1944 led to the destruction of almost the entire Third Panzer Army. Could this collapse have been prevented? If not, could the extent of the defeat have been much less?

The operational intentions that we believed the Soviets harboured have been discussed in detail. We had laid them out in our assessment of the situation on 11 May, and had reiterated our concerns on several other occasions. Specifically, we expected that two enemy armies would strike the left wing of the panzer army and would head towards the southwest. We also expected a simultaneous attack by at least two armies against the right wing of the panzer army which would drive deep into the flank of the Fourth Army. It was likely that the enemy planned to carry out a pincer attack in order to eliminate the Fourth Army and the Third Panzer Army, after which he would advance further west. Vitebsk had in this case lost its operational significance, for the enemy would not want the bulk of his forces to be committed and tied down to the city.

Our suspicions were confirmed by the concentration of Soviet troops on either side of Vitebsk at the end of May and at the beginning of June. The German supreme command was oblivious to what might come out of this build-up. No reserves were allocated to the Third Panzer Army. Army Group Centre saw itself as unable to help, so it seemed as if the panzer army was supposed to give itself freedom of action by creating reserves from its own forces. But this could not be done, for we were forbidden to make the decision to withdraw to the Tiger Line. Vitebsk had been designated a fortress. Half of the divisions of the panzer army were thereby assigned to a sector of the front against which the Soviets would probably refrain from launching an attack. It is open to question as to whether the commander of Army Group Centre, Field-Marshal Ernst Busch, was making these decisions himself or whether he was acting under Hitler's orders. This question shall not be examined here.

Over the course of several months, we had expressed our reservations about the Vitebsk fortress to the army group (verbally on a number of occasions and in writing twice). We had always highlighted what was bound to ensue. Our proposals to abandon Vitebsk in a timely manner and to establish a defensive position along the Tiger Line were always dismissed.

From the middle of May, there had been increasing signs that a major offensive would take place on either side of Vitebsk. In the last third of the month, we learnt from Soviet prisoners and deserters that the enemy was reinforcing his units on a large scale in the Vitebsk sector, especially in the area to the east of the city. A captured officer testified that there was one railway junction through which 35,000 men had been transported in the space of 14 days. We knew of one division whose strength had been increased by 2,000 of these men. The 5th Guards Rifle Corps of the 39th Army had been pulled out of its position east of Vitebsk and had been sent to the southern front of the breakthrough area, far to the west of the Vitebsk–Orsha road. Further east on this same southern front, the 5th Army placed its point of main effort in the Sukhodrovka sector. Our aerial reconnaissance had noticed a rise in movement along the Smolensk–Liozno railway line. It was calculated that 13 rifle divisions had been brought to the front along this railway line in the period from 28 May to 14 June. But we had to assume that the number of enemy units was much higher, for the slow movement on this line would have meant the probable disembarkation of the motor-ised troops in the Smolensk area. We could be certain of the presence of a guards army and of sizeable armoured forces. The only surprise for us was that these armoured forces turned out to be the entire 5th Guards Tank Army.

The enemy was reconnoitring the terrain, creating bridgeheads, and digging trenches along the frontline. He was conducting local combat to consolidate a jump-off position. There were constant indications from POW statements and spy reports of the arrival of guards troops. Tanks and artillery were also moving in, with our aerial photographs revealing 130 batteries with 480 guns in a concentrated area. All of this clearly told us that the enemy sought to launch a decisive strike from the area southeast of Vitebsk.

The situation was similar to the northwest of the city. We first spotted here the arrival of a complete armoured unit. The 6th Guards Army was detached from the front before our left neighbour (the Sixteenth Army) and was sent to the Nevel area, so we could expect that it would be used against the left wing of the Third Panzer Army. Large parts of the Red Air Force shifted their focus to this area. The 43rd Army, which had been distributed along the northeast side of the Vitebsk salient, relocated its point of main effort around Lake Zaronovskoye (northwest of the city). We also observed two new divisions here. There remained only five rifle divisions around the rest of the salient.

Other signs of an imminent attack from the area northwest of Vitebsk lay in the overwhelming presence of fighter aircraft, the increase in the number of artillery units (especially around Sirotino), and the considerable expenditure of ammunition by this artillery. The enemy was also reconnoitring the terrain and manoeuvring his infantry into position.

We reported our observations daily to those 'above'. There was clear proof that the Soviets were preparing to advance from the two areas they had carved out through the winter battles, i.e. from the southeast and from the northwest of Vitebsk. The extent of their preparations indicated an operational objective far beyond the encirclement of the city. They would break through towards the west, overrun and annihilate the Third Panzer Army from the north and south, and then advance towards East Prussia and the Baltic states. This objective would be decisive for the outcome of the war!

With what could the panzer army oppose the enemy? He had gathered together the 5th and 39th Armies, amounting to 20 divisions, southeast of Vitebsk, and this was before the arrival of the 5th Guards Tank Army.

Yet the panzer army had only three divisions in this vicinity with which to mount a defence. Northwest of the city, the enemy had assembled the 43rd Army and the 4th Shock Army, as well as the 6th Guards Army from the Nevel area, for his advance. We had just two divisions. Our Sixth Air Fleet reported that the enemy had complete mastery of the skies. The front of the panzer army was 180 kilometres in length. It was covered by only nine infantry divisions, of which four or five were pinned down along the curved front of the Vitebsk salient. Each battalion had approximately 300 men, creating an average of 102 men per kilometre of frontline.

Aside from the vast numerical inferiority of the panzer army, there was also a significant shortage of weaponry. What we had was insufficient to defend against a major offensive. Our artillery was weak, and there was an inadequate quantity of armour-piercing weapons. We were convinced that, in addition to the bravery and endurance of our soldiers, the substantial allotment of army artillery, assault guns, rocket projectors, and armour-piercing weapons had tilted both winter defensive battles in our favour. In view of the upcoming defensive battle, which was bound to be most difficult, it was quite incomprehensible to us that we were now equipped with only six army artillery battalions and a small number of assault guns, tanks, and armour-piercing weapons. There were no rocket projectors.

We could safely assume that there would be little offensive action against the Vitebsk salient. Even so, we had been ordered to allow three divisions to be encircled around the city. This was a complete waste of our forces. At this moment, five Soviet divisions and a so-called 'fortification zone' (manned by a defensive task force) stood opposite our four divisions.

As already described, we frequently reported to the army group our opinion of and counterproposals to the Vitebsk fortress. We particularly made the point that the divisions committed to the fortress would tie down only very few Soviet forces and would be more urgently needed for our defence against the imminent major offensive. We reported the activity to the southeast of Vitebsk on a daily basis. There could be no doubt that an attack would be launched from there. Our reports on the situation to the northwest of the city were just as frequent, so we also expected an attack on the largest scale from that location. Our warnings fell on deaf ears. We were told – unofficially – to stop grumbling about the fortress. Nonetheless, we continued to report our observations and objections.

An explanation for the failure of the supreme command to comprehend the operational intentions of the Soviets in the area of Vitebsk can perhaps be found in the petering out of our sources of information on the enemy. German announcements on the radio and in the press about our successful monitoring of Soviet radio messages encouraged the enemy to stop his radio traffic altogether, especially that of the guards, tank, mortar, and pioneer units. Thanks to our ground and aerial reconnaissance, we were able to put together, most arduously, a complete picture of Soviet offensive preparations. Furthermore, it cannot be denied that the supreme command had its gaze firmly focused on enemy activity before Army Group South and Army Group North Ukraine, so it may have been unable to pay enough attention to such activity on the front of the Third Panzer Army.

At any rate, the panzer army would have to await the enemy pincer attack with the forces currently at its disposal, of which half were regrettably committed in the Vitebsk salient. In our opinion, it was absolutely necessary to evacuate Vitebsk and to fall back to the Tiger Line. Taking into account the lake-dotted terrain along this line, the front of the panzer army would be shortened by 70 kilometres. This would have enabled one or two divisions to be put on standby in panzer army reserve. Sufficient infantry reserves could be detached and used to reinforce defensive combat, the defensive power of our artillery and armour could be doubled, and the measures needed for defensive and counteroffensive action could be taken.

Yet what would have been most decisive is that, upon reaching the Tiger Line, we would have been able to withdraw a substantial portion of our forces and make them available, from the outset, for the upcoming defensive fighting. At the time, we thought that three divisions could make such a withdrawal, but in hindsight it could have been four or even five. From this line, the panzer army would have survived the defensive battle without additional help. At the very least, it can be safely assumed that the Soviets would not have penetrated the Tiger Line as quickly as they eventually did after 22 June on either side of Vitebsk. A great deal of time would have therefore been gained, and even the supreme command would have become convinced that the assessment by the panzer army of the enemy's strength and intentions had been correct. Reinforcements would have been sent promptly to the panzer army. Even better would have been to provide the panzer army with a fully mobile reserve (a motorised or panzer division) for the defence along the Tiger Line. Only then would we have been in a position to conduct operations successfully against a rapidly moving enemy.

The panzer army would have obtained the advantage over the enemy had it retreated to the Tiger Line. There were a number of natural obstacles along the length of this line, including several lakes and the Western Dvina, so it would have offered us a particularly favourable position from which to defend ourselves. It had been constructed with great determination over the course of many months. The front of the Vitebsk salient was approximately 110 kilometres in length; the Tiger Line was only two thirds as long, although in practice it was much shorter, that is, with the lakes taken into consideration.

A withdrawal of the front to this line on 21 June, the day before that on which we expected the major offensive, would have thrown all Soviet arrangements into disarray. The situation that the enemy expected to encounter upon the commencement of his attack would have changed instantly. Not only would the Soviets have had to reorganise their infantry and artillery, which by itself would have postponed the attack against the Tiger Line for several days; they would have also had to completely overhaul their offensive plan given that the new front would be composed of a chain of lakes and the Western Dvina. Finally, our rear guards would have been less exposed had we retreated to the Tiger Line. We would have been able to hold this line for some time, giving our supreme command the opportunity to fully appreciate the danger posed by the enemy.

We were thus compelled to go into battle on 22 June in the knowledge that the rejection of our recommendation had been a catastrophic mistake. The panzer army could not meet the demands of the approaching defensive battle on either side of Vitebsk. We had too few divisions available, with a shortage of both artillery and armour-piercing weapons. Our defensive sectors were wide and our forces were weak. We faced an enemy whose numbers were far greater than had been in the winter defensive battles. We were well aware, and had also frequently reported, that an encirclement of Vitebsk would lead to the loss of much more than four divisions. We had reported that these divisions would fail to tie down any noteworthy quantity of enemy forces and that, as a result of the loss of these divisions, a gap of 35 to 40 kilometres would inevitably appear in our front. We would then have no forces with which to close this gap. We went into battle with the greatest concern. All our hopes of surviving, of preventing an encirclement of Vitebsk, and of saving four or more divisions lay in the following: first, we had reinforced our defensive positions as much as we could; second, our leadership had proven itself in two heavy winter defensive battles; and, third, our troops were full of confidence because they remembered our successes in the winter and because they had fresh ammunition.

It did at least seem as if the army group had begun to attach greater credence to the assessment of the situation by the panzer army, for two divisions (unfortunately not mobile) from army group reserve were placed behind our front: the 95th Infantry Division in the central sector and the 14th Infantry Division on the boundary with our right-hand neighbour. Yet these divisions were of little value during the conduct of the defensive battle, for their immobility rendered them ineffective against the motorised and armoured forces of the enemy. An infantry division can only counterattack against an enemy breakthrough in close quarters when supported by defensive mobile forces and armour. An important precondition, though, is that it be in close proximity to the enemy's point of penetration. Otherwise, from experience, an infantry division can reinforce the defence by handing over individual battalions or regiments for smaller counterattacks. The divisional headquarters would only assume responsibility for its own sector once the bulk of its infantry is in use.

Although those 'above' had failed to order the withdrawal to the Tiger Line before the commencement of the offensive, they still had the opportunity to do so on the evening of 22 June at the latest. The commitment of the 6th Guards Army against the sector of the IX Corps had been verified by that point in time. Before then, a question mark had hung over whether it had been in the Nevel area. We recognised that the two divisions of the IX Corps would be incapable of holding out against such an overwhelmingly superior enemy formation. It was also apparent that the Soviets would begin their major offensive against the Sukhodrovka sector, southeast of Vitebsk, early on 23 June with strong armoured support, for our ground observation had already spotted 135 enemy tanks in that vicinity. Finally, by 22 June, it was clear that the enemy was dispersing his forces before the curved front of the Vitebsk salient, so we could expect that he would only be able to execute weak holding attacks in this sector. This showed, already, that the enemy had no intention of letting substantial forces be tied down by our divisions in Vitebsk.

We had firmly established that the enemy was building up his forces southeast and northwest of the city and that he was thinning out his forces around the curve of the salient. Had the panzer army been given freedom of action that very evening, the immediate abandonment of the Vitebsk fortress and the withdrawal of the front to a fully-developed position 15 kilometres southwest of the city would still have been possible. By rapidly carrying out this retreat, the panzer army would have been able, without support, to free up one or two divisions for the support of the corps on each wing. It would then have been possible, in the face of continuous enemy pressure, to fall back to the Tiger Line and maintain a coherent front until further reserves were allocated to us.

On this evening at the latest, the supreme command would have had to recognise that the purpose of the Vitebsk fortress — 'to act as a bulwark against the Soviet onslaught and to tie down strong forces' — no longer existed, for it was obvious that the enemy planned to bypass Vitebsk. He had long been aware of our intention of tying down his troops with fortresses. It was for this reason that he simply went around them, provided he did not immediately require them for their road and railway junctions. Such was the case for Vitebsk. Thanks to the dry summer weather, the enemy was not bound to the major roads. He had at his disposal the Orsha–Smolensk and the Nevel–Polotsk routes for his supply lines. We heard from several deserters and prisoners the following words: 'Vitebsk will just fall into the lap of the Soviets like fruit from a tree when it is ripe'. Yet, even now, this made no impression on those 'above'. Hitler's demand for fortresses, formerly called 'strongpoints', had been a good solution, perhaps even the only one, for stabilising the front in early 1942. The Soviets had soon understood the purpose of these strongpoints and had begun to bypass them. We had maintained them regardless. They had increasingly become an obsession of Hitler's and were costing us much, much blood.

Our aerial reconnaissance spotted the arrival of a large armoured formation in the area northwest of Vitebsk on 23 June. The enemy thereby possessed such superiority both southeast and northwest of the city that there was no way we could prevent him from penetrating deep into our territory. We were already certain, on this second day of battle, that his plan was to envelop Vitebsk from either side with a small proportion of his forces, leaving the bulk of his troops free to advance westwards. It was abundantly clear that the threatened encirclement of the LIII Corps would result not only in three, but perhaps even four or five divisions being cut off from the front. It was just as clear that the corps on each wing would be confronted by powerful enemy thrusts. Despite this, Hitler expressly ordered that the front around Vitebsk was to be held. Without being allowed to fall back to the Tiger Line, and without being assigned strong mobile reserves, the annihilation of the panzer army was unavoidable. We would then have little left with which to close the gap that would open up in the front.

It cannot be emphasised strongly enough that there were only two options we could pursue if we were to counter the Soviet summer offensive before its commencement. Either we had to position strong mobile reserves before the anticipated points of penetration or, if such reserves were unavailable, we had to give up Vitebsk and move back to the Tiger Line.

Neither of these options was pursued. We at the headquarters of the Third Panzer Army repeatedly pointed out to those at the headquarters of

Army Group Centre our numerical inferiority. We said it was necessary that we be reinforced with army artillery, tanks, rocket projectors, and antiaircraft guns. If not, we had to be permitted to retreat immediately. Yet not once after the beginning of the offensive, when the intentions of the enemy had become glaringly obvious, was the second (and now only) option pursued. Our hands were tied.

It was on 24 June that we had our last chance to at least partially salvage the situation. The LIII Corps, now loosely encircled in Vitebsk, and the 4th Luftwaffe Field Division, encircled in Ostrovno, could have made a united effort that evening to break through to the front of the panzer army. But this plan was dashed when Hitler ordered that the 206th Infantry Division remain in Vitebsk. By the time the LIII Corps sought to break out of the ring of encirclement (early on 26 June), the enemy had already tightened the noose around the city. He also held the Tiger Line with a reversed front, so there was no way in which we could succeed.

The ramifications of our lack of freedom of action during these critical days of combat were devastating. The Third Panzer Army was paralysed. Any retreat we proposed required the approval of the army group at the very least, but in most cases even the OKH, and therefore the Führer, became involved. We would often have to deal with a series of time-consuming queries. Hardly any order or decision of ours at this time did not require input from those 'above'. If we did manage to obtain the approval we needed, it would often be too late! And the order to break out of Vitebsk was too late.

To summarise, the men and their commanders had done everything they possibly could in preparation and in battle. The morale of the troops had been excellent. The reasons for the near-complete annihilation of the Third Panzer Army were as follows:

1. Our own weaknesses (a wide front, little artillery, and few armour-piercing weapons);
2. The overwhelming numerical superiority of the enemy, the degree of which was not appreciated by the supreme command until well after the commencement of the summer offensive;

3. The almost non-existent freedom of action given to the leadership of the Third Panzer Army;
4. The irresolution of the supreme command – decisions were often made when it was too late;
5. And above all, Hitler's order that the Vitebsk fortress be held by three divisions. Hitler's obsession with fortresses, even though they had lost their relevance two years previously, contributed decisively to the tragedy of the summer of 1944 and thus to our defeat in 1945.

The destruction of the Third Panzer Army within seven days ushered in this summer tragedy. The annihilation of the Ninth Army in the southern sector of Army Group Centre took place at roughly the same time. Between 22 June and 15 July 1944, the army group suffered shockingly high casualties (380,000 soldiers wounded, killed, or missing). This was a decisive defeat. Such losses could not be replaced.

Even if the supreme command had understood Soviet intentions in the vicinity of Vitebsk and had done a better job in allocating forces to the Third Panzer Army and in returning to it freedom of action, it cannot be conclusively asserted that it would have prevented the collapse of the panzer army and, in consequence, of Army Group Centre. Many sources concerning the events of the summer of 1944 remain inaccessible, and only once they are thoroughly examined can history reach a verdict. But there is one indisputable historical truth: the Third Panzer Army had endeavoured, even after the commencement of the enemy offensive, to stop the unfolding catastrophe. The soldiers of the panzer army had given their all in confronting the onslaught and in attempting to minimise the extent of the defeat.

The units under the command of the Third Panzer Army between May 1943 and June 1944

VI Corps
IX Corps, from 11 October 1943
XXXXIII Corps, until 14 September 1943
LIII Corps, from 30 September 1943
LIX Corps, until 10 September 1943
II Luftwaffe Field Corps, until 10 September 1943

12th Infantry Division, from 28 December 1943 until 16 February 1944
14th Infantry Division, from 22 September 1943
24th Infantry Division, from 22 June 1944
83rd Infantry Division, until 14 September 1943
87th Infantry Division, until 5 February 1944
95th Infantry Division, from 5 February 1944
129th Infantry Division, from 6 October 1943 until 22 January 1944
131st Infantry Division, from 30 December 1943 until 16 March 1944
197th Infantry Division, from 18 December 1943
205th Infantry Division, until 14 September 1943
206th Infantry Division
211th Infantry Division, from 10 November 1943 until 28 February 1944
212th Infantry Division, from 28 June 1944

246th Infantry Division, from 25 September 1943
252nd Infantry Division, from 4 November 1943
256th Infantry Division, from 27 September 1943
263rd Infantry Division, until 14 September 1943
290th Infantry Division, from 24 June 1944
291st Infantry Division, until 17 September 1943
299th Infantry Division, from 31 December 1943
330th Infantry Division, until September 1943
5th Jäger Division, from 25 December 1943 until 6 March 1944
Corps Detachment D, from 17 February 1944
2nd Luftwaffe Field Division, disbanded October 1943
3rd Luftwaffe Field Division, disbanded 22 January 1944
4th Luftwaffe Field Division
6th Luftwaffe Field Division
20th Infantry Division (motorised), until 18 July 1943
8th Panzer Division, until July 1943
12th Panzer Division, from 4 January until 22 January 1944
20th Panzer Division, from 10 October 1943
Panzer-Grenadier Division Feldherrnhalle, from 20 December 1943 until 17 January 1944
Combat group of the 18th Panzer-Grenadier Division, from 14 November 1943
Divisional staff of the 36th Infantry Division, until 25 October 1943
Divisional staff of the 113th Infantry Division, until 10 December 1943
Headquarters of the 18th Brigade, for special use, until 11 February 1944
1st SS Infantry Brigade (motorised), until 26 June 1943
201st Security Division
211th Security Division, temporarily from 11 November 1943
391st Field Training Division, until 13 January 1944

Obstacle-Construction Unit von Wagner (Jürgen) and Obstacle-Construction Group Eckhardt, winter 1943/44
Obstacle-Construction Unit Boehnesch of the Fourth Army, from 13 December 1943 until 12 January 1944
Combat Group von Gottberg, winter 1943/44

4th Air Division
18th Flak Division (headquarters of the 6th Flak Regiment, 2nd Battalion of the 49th Flak Regiment, 93rd Light Flak Battalion)

1st, 2nd, 4th, 5th, and 7th Jäger Battalions
Panzer Army Service School
550th Infantry Battalion, for special use
609th Security Regiment
335th, 343rd, 480th, 557th, 564th, 579th, 591st, 663rd, 722nd, 795th, 797th, 839th, 860th, and 989th Security Battalions
231st, 330th, and 860th Reserve Rifle Battalions
2nd and 24th SS Police Regiments
1st Battalion of the 3rd Brandenburg Regiment
Third Panzer Army Assault Battalion
9th, 11th, and 15th Field Penal Battalions
2nd Bicycle Security Regiment
7th, 8th, 28th, and 53rd Military Police Companies
57th Auxiliary Police Battalion

313th Special Staff Artillery Officer
Headquarters of the 618th, 775th, and 788th Artillery Regiments, for special use
427th, 506th, 635th, 808th, 816th, 845th, 846th, 848th, 859th, and 990th Heavy Army Artillery Battalions
426th and 430th Light Artillery Battalions
601st and 635th Howitzer Battalions
126th, 139th, 148th, and 502nd Artillery Commanders
2nd Battalion of each of the 39th, 41st, 47th, 61st, 64th, 66th, and 68th Artillery Regiments
423rd Light Artillery Battalion
9th and 15th Light Artillery Observation Battalions
45th, 46th, and 54th Frontline Artillery Observation Battalions

501st and 505th Heavy Panzer Battalions (Tigers)
519th and 655th Heavy Panzerjäger Battalions (Hornets)

664th and 742nd Heavy Panzerjäger Battalions
177th, 189th, 190th, 237th, 245th, 281st, 300th, 600th, 667th, 909th, 1014th, and 1195th Assault-Gun Battalions (from February 1944: Assault-Gun Brigades)

Headquarters of the 4th Rocket Projector Brigade
51st and 53rd Rocket Projector Regiments
2nd Heavy Rocket Projector Regiment

High Command of the 8th Pioneer Battalion, for special use
Headquarters of the 7th Fortress Pioneer Battalion
743rd and 745th Army Pioneer Battalions
54th and 208th Bridge Pioneer Battalions (motorised)
18th, 46th, 78th, 91st, 97th, 103rd, 123rd, 136th, 213th, 214th, 222nd, 415th, and 420th Construction Pioneer Battalions
Bridge Columns K 62, B 89, B 1./411, J 845, B 867, B 869
Heavy Panzer Bridge Column 849
Headquarters of the 9th, 513th, 546th, and 628th Pioneer Regiments
42nd, 62nd, and 505th Pioneer Regiments (motorised)
7th Fortress Pioneer Battalion
644th Fortress Battalion
730th, 731st, 732nd, 784th, 794th, and 796th Frontline Construction Pioneer Battalions
Commander of the 1st Battalion of the 1st Railway Pioneer Regiment
139th Railway Construction Battalion
Organisation Todt Superior Construction Command 'Elbe'
Organisation Todt Line Chief 9

Third Panzer Army Signal Regiment
703rd and 710th Secret Field Police Groups
8th Signal Intelligence Battalion
46th, 49th, and 453rd Corps Signal Battalions
113th, 210th, and 318th Panzer Messenger Detachments
697th Panzer Propaganda Company

615th Antiaircraft Battalion
295th Army Antiaircraft Battalion
Antiaircraft Cavalry Regiment Centre

Armoured Trains 61 and 67
Track Protection Trains 'Werner' and 'Blücher'

Affidavit on anti-bandit warfare[1]

Otto Heidkämper
Lieutenant-General (retired)

27 June 1946

I, Lieutenant-General Otto Heidkämper, being duly sworn, depose and say:

'Affidavit'

I was chief of staff of the Third Panzer Army, first as colonel on the general staff and then as major-general, under Colonel-General Reinhardt between 3 May 1943 and 17 August 1944.

---

[1]Translator's note: This statement was written by Otto Heidkämper in 1946 as evidence for the Nuremberg trials. While not in Heidkämper's original book, it is included in this translation because it concerns the anti-partisan warfare waged by the Third Panzer Army in 1943 and 1944. For the German-language text, see *Trial of the Major War Criminals before the International Military Tribunal, Nuremberg, 14 November 1945–1 October 1946: Volume XLII*, Nuremberg, 1949, pp. 258–261.

Re: anti-bandit warfare

(a) Atrocities

In the period during which the Third Panzer Army was defending Vitebsk (i.e. between May 1943 and June 1944), the murder of members of the panzer army by bandits behind the front and in the rear area of the panzer army was the order of the day. Almost all of the murdered German soldiers were robbed and, for the most part, dreadfully mutilated.

The bandit warfare in the area of the Third Panzer Army, because of the dogged and malicious fanaticism with which the bandits fought, is not to be compared with the honourable combat of the soldiers on the frontline. Our soldiers constantly found their comrades murdered and brutally mutilated by the bandits, so it was inevitable that the anti-bandit struggle would become increasingly bitter and ruthless. A significant contributing factor to this was the fact that the bandits, whenever their fight seemed to have become hopeless, chose to behave most treacherously. If our soldiers approached to take prisoners, the bandits, who had supposedly surrendered, would open fire with all their rifles and machine guns – wanton murder.

The bandits would frequently wait in water or in swamps, or would bury themselves in the ground, and, for hours on end, they would draw air through the neck of a broken bottle. They would allow German soldiers to pass by and would then murder them from behind.

(b) Army field orders

Because of these recurring incidents, the troops engaged in anti-bandit warfare repeatedly expressed to Colonel-General Reinhardt the desire to ignore the provisions of The Hague Convention, for such provisions were not in any way adhered to by the bandits. Reinhardt rejected this request. To respond to murder with murder was incompatible with his religious disposition and his sense of honour as a German officer. I know how my commander suffered emotionally every time one of his soldiers was murdered by the bandits and how he often wrestled with himself over the question of whether to allow his men to exact retribution. His decision was the same on every occasion: 'It is the same as before. We want to remain decent soldiers.' He told the commanders and their subordinates during his daily visits to the front that they were always to remain civilised, even when conducting anti-bandit operations.

Before every anti-bandit operation, the high command of the Third Panzer Army would issue written orders as to how captured bandits were to be led away. It was specifically ordered – whether written or orally I no longer know – that those bandits who were overcome in combat or who were taken after surrendering were to be treated in exactly the same way as captured soldiers were. Those who were wounded were to receive medical attention. They were even admitted to the military hospitals for the troops of the Eastern Army.

In accordance with the orders of the panzer army, every captured bandit was to be questioned before being led away. A bandit who was found indisputably guilty of murdering a German soldier was to be shot immediately after a summary court-martial. Nevertheless, most of the bandits who were burdened with such guilt committed suicide beforehand. The rest were handed over, as we had been ordered, to be used as labourers in Germany. The troops were in full cry over this measure, for they did not understand why such malicious bandits and suspected murderers should be deported to the Fatherland as workers. They argued over and over that captured bandits should be employed for dangerous tasks near the front (mine sweeping and ammunition transportation). This proposal was discussed in a telephone conversation between Colonel-General Reinhardt and Field-Marshal von Kluge, the commander in chief of Army Group Centre, sometime in August 1943, but it was rejected. Captured bandits would continue to be sent to the Reich.

(c) Violation of rights

There are no known cases of German soldiers violating the rights of bandits. In accordance with the orders of Colonel-General Reinhardt, we took appropriate action in dealing with them.

(d) Official punishments and hostages

Amidst the violence and atrocities committed by the bandits, there was no instance in which the high command of the Third Panzer Army punished the population or took hostages. The troops often indicated in writing that the population living near the front and in the areas endangered by bandits frequently provided assistance to the Germans. The population had nothing in common with the bandits, and our troops requested that their goods and chattels, as well as their lives, be spared. The population in the bandit-controlled territories had been constantly called upon by leaflets we released from the sky to leave these areas; otherwise, there was the possibility that they themselves would be regarded as bandits in upcoming German operations. In the event, despite these warnings, our men still treated as non-combatants those who had remained. So long as their livestock was not required locally for the provision of food to the combat troops, this population, on the order of the Third Panzer Army, was resettled with their livestock and their movable belongings outside the territory that had been controlled by the bandits.

List of Heidkämper's sources
for *Vitebsk*

Daily reports from the headquarters of the Third Panzer Army to Army
Group Centre, 1943/44
Extracts from the war diary of the Third Panzer Army
Copies of documents and orders of the Third Panzer Army
Intelligence reports of the Third Panzer Army
Author's maps from the winter battles of 1943/44 and from the Soviet
summer offensive of 1944
Diary notes from Colonel-General Reinhardt and from the author
Author's notes and letters

Statements about the enemy and his strength are based on the information available to the Third Panzer Army in 1943/44.

Index